A Welsh Eye

By the same author

NOVELS

Where Did I Put My Pity?
The Alone To The Alone
The World Cannot Hear You
Frost On My Frolic
Point Of Order
The Love Man
The Dark Philosophers
All Things Betray Thee
Now Lead Us Home
The Stranger At My Side
Gazooka
Ring Delirium 123
The Lusty Lobby
The Sky Of Our Lives

PLAYS

The Keep
Loud Organs
Jackie The Jumper

NON-FICTION

A Few Selected Exits

A WELSH EYE

by Gwyn Thomas

Drawings by John Dd. Evans

HUTCHINSON

London Melbourne Sydney Auckland Johannesberg

Hutchinson & Co. (Publishers) Ltd

An imprint of the Hutchinson Publishing Group

17-21 Conway Street, London WIP 6JD

Hutchinson Group (Australia) Pty Ltd
30-32 Cremorne Street, Richmond South, Victoria 3121
PO Box 151, Broadway, New South Wales 2007

Hutchinson Group (NZ) Ltd
32-34 View Road, PO Box 40-086, Glenfield, Auckland 10

Hutchinson Group (SA) Pty Ltd
PO Box 337, Bergvlei 2012, South Africa

First published 1964
First published as a Hutchinson Paperback 1984
© Gwyn Thomas 1964
Illustrations © Hutchinson & Co. (Publishers) Ltd 1964

Printed and bound in Great Britain by Anchor Brendon Ltd
Tiptree, Essex

ISBN 0 09 154061 5

Acknowledgements

Extracts from *The Collected Poems of W. H. Davies* and *The Autobiography of a Super Tramp* are quoted by kind permission of Mrs H. M. Davies and the publishers, Jonathan Cape Ltd.

The chapter 'A Thought for the Dragon' originally appeared in a shortened version in *Punch*, with whose kind permission it is published again in this book.

Contents

1   The Central Wound   9

2   Bards, Regrets and the Restless Spirit   25

3   Revivalism and the Falling Larks   39

4   The Way to the Sea   57

5   Self-Improvement   69

6   A Clutch of Perished Bards   88

7   A Thought for the Dragon   103

8   Dusk and the Dialectic   112

9   Devotions   122

10 Cardiff and her Smaller Sisters   135

11 West and Up   160

1 The Central Wound

COME up towards the Rhondda from Llantrisant. The hills grow less gentle. The fields lose grace and lushness. The first coal tips sit fatly on torn slopes. Black pyramids set up by nimble-witted Pharaohs who had the theatrical guile not to get themselves enclosed within. The housing takes on the sombre, barrack-like monotony that even has the mice complaining and keeps the average modern architect in a deep faint and glad to be there. Pass Tonyrefail. You'll pass it if you survive that astonishing slope on the edge of the town. So many cars have stalled on this place that many people of the district still think that Ford backed a loser, and even goats have been known to knock on the vet's door with a burned gear-box after tackling it.

Then you reach the broad, reedy moorland, the Waun. It is a gaunt place, this, a lonely place where even ravens and gulls have a way of trading crumbs for nerve tonic. And beyond the Waun, the great barrier ridge that marks the southern limit of the Rhondda. There is a deep hostile stare about that wall of grey and green. These mountains do not like what has been done to them. Too much has been taken from them. They proclaim it in sight and sound. Their rims are shot through with outbreaks of defensive rock and most of the winds that blow off them are husky with recollections of storm, outrage and ancient battles that nobody could possibly have won.

We come to the crown of the ridge. Here on one side is the road to Tonypandy, sharply, abidingly to the left. Straight ahead, across the deep bowl in which Porth stands is Penrhiwgwynt mountain. It is curiously pastoral with its lay-out of many coloured fields. From our kitchen window we could see the fringe of trees on its top. They were small trees, tilted back by the winds from the sea. They suggested gasps of astonishment, as if they had taken one look at Porth when they got tall

9

A Southern bastion
of the Rhondda

enough and had been trying to get away ever since. From Porth the spokes of terraces and work-places shoot up to Treorchy and Maerdy, and down south to Pontypridd. Society and nature have come together here to achieve some amazing patterns and they should be told not to do it again.

And between Porth and Trebanog lies my village, Cymmer. My life between two and ten years of age wore itself wild and bandy-legged on that fierce and fascinating slope. You'll pardon my harping on this question of gradients, but the lack of flatness between Porth and Trebanog was a thematic thing in our lives. Before the buses came there were elderly people by the score rusted down by habit or rheumatism who stuck to their kitchens and never ventured from Trebanog or Upper Cymmer down into Porth. The walk down was one thing but it was not always easy to recruit somebody to push you back up a gradient of two in three, and the rickshaw service, with so much time given over to digging and singing, was patchy.

The day the bus service started up through Cymmer and Trebanog and Tonyrefail was an occasion of excitement and meaning. We children had turned out as if for some climactic summer treat, dressed in our best and in a vocal trim to blow the bus up that mortal phase of the slope if the wheels, for some reason or another, vanished in Lower Trebanog. They had mobilised some of the saddest and least active of the elderly population, and they were installed in the bus for the pioneer trip. The first journeyers to the moon will look no tenser than that little phalanx of adventurers. The bus roared into action. We ran as a body just behind it, singing for joy, touching the glossy red paint and getting drunk in the petrol fumes.

A fussy councillor, regretting the calm of the horse age, kept shouting, 'Back, children, back. It may slip. This is a juggernaut.' As we chugged through mid-Cymmer, and we had now switched from singing to mimicking perfectly the bus's every noise, a woman, whose voice had once been a golden legend in the lower Rhondda, leaned out of the bus to a point where she could have kissed the pavement and had two panicky passengers hanging on to each leg. She bawled to some relations and friends, 'Wave to me. I'm in a bus.' And no one had ever stood a better chance of suddenly not being so.

But gaiety turned to something like terror when the machine approached the foot of Farmer's Hill. The engine coughed and snorted as if it were trying to get out and walk. A local sage, Waldo Aberystwyth, gave the driver a most distracting tap and asked him if Rolls and Ford

Rhondda Barrier Ridge

had been told of this particular gradient up to Trebanog before exposing humanity to this nonsense of internal combustion.

To the left of the hill's peak is the field where the Rugby team recruited from Cymmer and Trebanog used to play. It was the least level pitch in Christendom. Those who survived it got a diploma from Darwin. It was the only Rugby field where the players were allowed to dip their bits of lemon in adrenalin while sitting in an oxygen tent at half-time, and the referee was allowed to call in a relative or use a motor horn if he lacked the breath to make the pea move inside the metal. The Trebanog and Cymmer boys mastered the slope. They were badly defeated but once and then the victors were found to have two Sherpas on the wing on loan from Tibet.

Most of the houses in Cymmer are of the traditional cottage type endemic in our mining villages. They were built in blocks of forty to fifty, each block large enough to evolve a personality, a culture, a pattern of stars and scars, all its own. In many of them the structure was flimsy to the point of being flippant. Start hammering in the top house and somebody was hanging on to the looser fittings in the bottom one.

How tiny and inadequate most of the houses look now. Like units in a game of blocks in a House of Correction. Take our kitchen. To the eye of childhood it had the size of the Albert Hall and the converging tumults of Crewe. We were not content to be a large number of brothers. We had a phalanx of friends who loved my sister's cooking. On a good day it was like an overflow meeting from Doctor Barnado's. Today its walls are about an inch away from my shoulders and the loud bustling cormorants have fled.

But the eye returning to this place sees most acutely the things, the great meaningful things that the years have led into silence. The rubbery, flaming-eyed band of tireless young yahoos with whom I romped through High Street, Graigwen, Lincoln and Argyll Streets, have gone and their games have been replaced by antics which I do not at once recognise as play. The huge colliery in the middle of the village, its rich, sinister heart, finished work in the late thirties. Just behind our house was the vast tip built up from the endless honeycombing of pitwork beneath us. The rattle of trams up and down the tip, through the day and notably through the night, clad each of our dreams in a cloak of sharp and cruel omens.

When we played on the tip it was jet-black, proud and growing. The engine-house at its top, which played out the hauling cable, was full of wheels that sang wonderful velvet, greasy songs. In those days we did not notice the tip's colour, its blasphemous lack of green. The young are great acceptors and the tip, like the pit, was the centre of our world. But grass of a sort grows over it now, a dim, grudging grass over the dramatic undulations, like a landscape of the moon. The old tracks of the tram-lines down its flank are a contracting, sardonic furrow. The engine-house is now an empty shell upon its eminence. The winds blow through it and the ferns creep back into their old kingdom.

We had no cinema in Cymmer itself. Our place of pilgrimage on a Saturday afternoon was The Grand or The Dog as we knew it. It was not difficult, with some hastily done chore on a Saturday morning, in my case the cleaning of cutlery for a family of twelve, to get the penny admission to The Grand. But there was another method that had a yard more panache to it. It was to take a couple of jars to the jam factory next door and get a penny on each. We followed the example of the hard boys of the upper age group whose fad was to buy with the second penny a fresh batch of bread and a swede. And we, with limping baby jaws, did likewise. The racket of that swede-chewing was immense. When the talkies came the clients had to agree to synchronise their dental swing to let an odd line of the dialogue through to the critics in the back.

Not long ago I looked at the dun, padlocked doors of that palace of delight. I think I could have stood before the Parthenon and felt relatively blithe, for the gods of the Greeks did not cry through my childhood. But in The Dog, locked up there, huge and articulate phantoms, were a countless parade of evenings that had shaped the eventual pattern of my mind, whatever it is. I was taken there for the first time by the daughter of a neighbour, a lovable but remiss maiden and daft on the pictures. I was about eighteen months old at the time. The temporary nurse had wrapped a shawl around me and I, as a male, had escorted her into the cinema. She stood in one of the side aisles, gawking at the epic being currently unrolled. It was a naval film. Some of it I saw over the shawl. Some of it I saw through the shawl. Good sight or poor shawl. The memory of that evening has stood so vividly by me through the years that I cannot even think of the navy or see the sea without having a strong taste of wool on my lips.

And in the middle of Cymmer is the chapel. A large chapel. Off-hand I would say one of the largest in the Rhondda, a place where piety has begotten more shapes in wood and stone than anywhere else in Britain. Of that chapel I was a member. Theologically, as a child, I had a tangled time of it. I was one of the Rhondda generation whose language, with an almost malignant ease, had changed from Welsh to English. But the chapel's teaching had remained in Welsh. I and my mentors blinked at each other across a wider gulf of heretical overtones than anything since Luther. But I cannot look at that building with anything but a deep, good love. For music does not concern itself with the base Machiavellianism of doctrine and vocabulary. Nations are torn apart, languages fall silent but the young will always sing. We could all learn enough Welsh to give a unique passion to the hymns we sang at the festivals of Easter and Whitsun.

And if Cymmer produced nothing else it was an abundance beyond praise of beautiful sunlit voices, soprano and especially alto. I say 'especially' because it was in that brazen section of the juvenile gallery that I and my brothers found ourselves. The chapel is now abandoned. Mice and the odd mutter of subsidence pronounce their own coda on the packed festivals of yesteryear. But in those days when it knew our triumphs of innocence and immaculate harmony, our Easter mornings of voices arising and hearts fulfilled, it and the men and women who made it raised a banner of loveliness and joy.

Now let's go back up the hill again. Down that side street to the left is the Library and Institute. There I had my first taste of what have been the great merits of life. Masses of books, good talk, concerts. There of a Sunday evening the Cymmer Military Band would play under their impressive bearded bandmaster, Mr Martin. He was a grave, Moses-like figure and it would never have surprised me to see his sheet music turn into tablets of stone. And there, too, in the draughts- and chess-room I sat in the company of sage and outrageous wags who seemed to see themselves merely as part of a vast cosmic jest. Those lads set my thoughts swinging to a satirical chime that will never be amended.

Just over to the left is St John's Hall which for years shuttled between being a centre for grand opera and the headquarters of the Ministry of Labour, both in those days demanding large casts and sombre synopses. And slightly higher up is the old graveyard. The earth of this musty and haunting patch was torn out of plumb by subsidence years before my time. The memorial tablets are painfully aslant and stare at each other in the most overt confusion. After a fairly jumpy life we thought the least a citizen can expect is a stable headstone.

Further along the road is the chip shop that was the hub of the late winter evenings. It was a place bulging with light, warmth and turbulent gossip. Often, in the intervals of waiting, clutches of junior artists fresh from the Band of Hope and vestry rehearsals and hot with a sense of worldly carousal, were recruited and hoisted on to the lemonade boxes and asked to sing. My own strong suit was songs of tender yearning and such sweetness I was accused more than once of taking the tang off the vinegar. I also had a batch of ballads from Sankey and Moody that would have moved a mule to remorse. With 'Have Courage My Boy To Say No' I was always sure of a bag of hot scrumps. With 'Where Is My Wandering Boy Tonight?' I got a cutlet to go with them.

A few weeks ago I walked around the green patch by the old steam fan where we played and talked and ate the lotus through the fat, delicious summers of childhood. I stopped to watch some boys playing. I pondered the violent tumble of events that had shattered the face of reality between my birth and theirs. One of them said, 'I wonder what he wants.'

So do I.

*   *   *

And now, in the closed mind what are the voices, the visions that continue to hang about?

Most of them are bound to relate to the period when the whole region seemed to be teetering on the edge of violence. The swift decline of economic power after the First World War had given a spearhead of fanatical decision to the vague, evangelical socialism and syndicalism that had formed the South Welsh political idiom since the beginning of the century.

Even around my cradle I seemed to detect angry fists and raised voices. The miners and their masters had elected to tear the entrails out of each other. About this there was nothing new. For a hundred years the valleys had been given over to industries that were brutally dangerous and dirty, with repression and revolt glaring at each other like imbecile twins. My gripe-water was flavoured with chopped pamphlets. As a pre-sleep tactic, my father would let me stroke a slight lump on the back of his head. This, he claimed, had been caused by some ruffianly cossack of a constable who had broken his truncheon on my father's pate during the Tonypandy Riots.

My elder brothers, bitter myth-deflaters to a man, swore that the contusion had been caused by a thrown coconut during a drunken revel at Barry Island. But I accepted my father's story and gave him my full sympathy when he rattled off the names of at least six men who had got on to the Council merely for having been within earshot of the riot.

The great strikes of 1921 and 1926 still operate as massive traumas in the less public parts of my psyche. In 1921 some Whitehall Napoleon dispatched a force of infantry, the Yorks and Lancs, to nip insurrection in the bud and protect the rentiers and virgins of the land from spoliation. The soldiers were small, unsoldierly and amorous fellows. Copulation throve and in our boyish games among the ferns, tripping over lovers and the attendant troupe of telescope-toting *voyeurs* became a fixed hazard. Often one would see a passionate Lancastrian being harangued by one of the miners appealing to him not to exhaust utterly the local supplies of warmth and to revert, for pity's sake, to the role of running dog of imperialism.

Through that summer we were fed in soup-kitchens, housed for the most part, and for the extra laugh, in vestries. The diet differed from that of a gaol only in being served by smiling and splendid women. Never was the sweet tooth of youth so thwarted. Soup bombarded with monstrous doughboys was the dish of the day. And this was usually followed by a type of tough, unsugared rice pudding which was later taken over by Japan as the Mark One of their buna product, synthetic rubber.

Off and on some jesting sadist would run around the village shouting, 'Fruit salad down the vestry.' We would swoop like gulls around the gates of the kitchens and watch the conventional two acres of rice being lifted out of the ovens. This may earn me a frown from the American Senate but there was Russian money behind this flow of dainties. The miners of the Don Basin had a whip-round and sent the valleys a cheque to the tune of 'Solidarity for Ever'.

The lady in charge was the colliery manager's wife. She would stand on a high platform, correcting our clumsier gaffes. Of these, the most frequent was to give our digestive tract a truce in the starch-war by sculpting a doughboy into a kind of Easter Island figurine. And occasionally she would, in a very clear voice, make an announcement that cut a permanent groove in my mind. 'Children, tomorrow you will bring your forks. There will be butter beans.' In that age there were a legion of tough things. Those butter beans came about fifth.

When the 1926 battle came around I was in the County School and outside the orbit of public charity. In most kitchens miracles of division and sharing swarmed like flies. The more astute got the middle cut of the sardine. Our earliest sexual stirrings were shadowed by so consistent a hunger that for years to come the zone's libido had a stammering tongue. The strike, begun in late spring, did not end until the autumn. The weather was flawless. Every day opened and closed like a great flower. The valley slipped back to its primal calm. The hillsides were murmurous with groups talking, singing, gambling with buttons or pins.

Disused Tip

At school every class witnessed a bijou but solemnly bitter civil war. The miners' sons were for conflict unto death. The sons of tradesmen and other people not affected by the fight were malignantly opposed to the whole business, especially during the General Strike part of the affray, when they had to go without buses and trains. They did the long walk down the valley, working up a fine, reactionary head of steam. I recall, one day, trying to explain to the son of a draper, a torpid, powerful boy, the content of a speech I had heard the night before in the concert room of the Library and Institute. The speaker had given us the exact shade and time of arrival of the Red Dawn. The draper's son listened patiently. He brooded over it for about a week. Then he asked me to repeat what I had said. I gave him the message once more, festooned with a few fresh Trotskyist axioms dredged up from the Institute. He hit me flat. Over the years the wound between us has healed somewhat. But even now I cannot be in his presence without feeling that the world is a little more fissile than it has the right to be.

The strikes left South Wales gutted and stricken. It is still difficult to assess the mind of Wales without reference to these outrageous collapses of the social framework. We saw lunacy established among us as an apparently normal stable companion. We saw, but we didn't quite believe. The experience left our imagination with a perpetual tilt towards the sardonic. Even in the current effervescence of new industry, the last product to be definitely marketed will be confidence. The geology of remembrance is damnably deep and will need to wait overlong for its final text-book. It will prove to be more insolent and unyielding than the rocks and destructive bubbling filth of this eroded and ambulant clinker. And legend has made our particular case more than usually complicated. Ever since the great battles in the North and Midlands of England that sent us haring towards Cardigan Bay, we have felt that east of Chepstow, Ross, Shrewsbury, stood a baleful and violent moron as ready to clobber us with penury in this century as he was to do it with battle-axes in the time of the Welsh princes.

The thirties gave South Wales their political peak. Coal, already a ruptured industry, had stepped down from first place as a battle cry. The world's brow was hot and we were out to fan it with banners. We suggested a possible definition of Wales as a non-stop protest with mutating consonants. Navels distended by resting banner-poles became one of the region's major stigmata. During the demonstrations against the Means Test and other bits of crass social legislation that put Britain in deep-freeze during the Baldwin period, we marched almost as a way

of life. We were trying to shout a little wisdom and compassion into the world's ear and the world was as deaf as a post.

Our slogans covered every contingency. Many banners would show a pair of staring eyes, indicating man's need of greater insight, and a pair of clasped hands, to symbolise unity. We must have been the first spot outside Asia to send warm greetings to Mao Tse-tung. Smaller causes would always find spokesmen. 'Keep Chepstow Welsh!' 'Remember Builth Wells!' 'Free Beer!' 'Hands off Cwmparc!' 'Keep Wales vocal!' 'Revive Tonic Sol Fa!' 'What about Colenso Jones?' This Colenso Jones was a paranoid bookmaker from Ferndale, who had accused the police of hounding him and his runners with undue zeal. He had been put away in an asylum and his case had overtones of the Dreyfus affair.

For the police were not loved in those days. They had a way of flipping you with their white gloves if groups of three or four stood on a pavement putting the comb through the world's tangled plight. And at all the major meetings, where you would nearly always get a fast gale of republican rage, anyone with a strong voice and a way of banging it like a torpedo against the back wall of the hall was nourished by the thinkers at the Institute with nuggets of information about every lapse in royal conduct all the way back to Ethelred and even further. And whenever they started beating out their Robespierre routine the constabulary, in their quaint Prussian-seeming helmets, could be seen making heavy weather of the shorthand notes that would help, later, to send one or more of the lads to stiffish terms in gaol. It is a cooling experience to see neighbours vanish into prison for the simple offence of frankness. The totally new relationship between people and police is as pleasant a sight as the factories that have sprouted on the disused tips of yesteryear. I never thought that they or I would make it.

The political marches were great musical occasions. The period that saw the incredible eruption of chapels witnessed also a vast spawning of bands. It was as if the darkening industrial context inspired a wish to react loudly. If life looks too insolently at you, blow back right in its face. If you have a euphonium to do it with, all the better. Whenever the multitudes thronged the valleys to suggest a sweeter ethic to the Herods of Whitehall, bands, their rehabilitated instruments reeking with metal polish, would come pouring from every street. It was the highest ratio of musician to marcher ever seen. And no two bands ever played in any related way. The band ahead of you might be splitting the sky with 'Colonel Bogey.' The one behind would be tenderly suggesting 'Hits from the Lilac Domino.'

In 1935 some climax of disgust brought the entire valley population on to the streets. As one watched the huge streams of protesters pouring up and down the two gulches on their way to Tonypandy, one could have sworn that the very blood of the place was on the boil. One of the visiting contingents was of members of the October Club, a very militant outfit at the University of Oxford. I had been a student there, on some of the most tenuous State-aid ever devised, until the previous year. The October boys called on me and requested that for Oxford's sweet sake, I should march behind their banner. I had to decline for I had already arranged to take my place with my large and entire family in the front ranks of the Porth phalanx. The Oxford boys were just behind. They had one band in front of them and one immediately behind. The conflicting tunes played hell with the rhythm of the afternoon. They were the only persons I have ever seen marching towards the New Jerusalem in strict waltz tempo.

Now the volcano lies still. The valleys now give out as little political clamour as those ghostly little villages of North Wales where slate was once quarried and lead mined. The banners have been furled and put away. A quieter, healing hedonism has set off a proliferation of bingo and drinking clubs as impressive in its way as the almost solid wall of conventicles and trade union lodges brought into being by the psychoses of poverty and dread. And just as well.

2 Bards, Regrets and the Restless Spirit

I DO not think it is possible to approach the National Eisteddfod as it stands today and make a fair judgment. If you have been exposed in childhood and youth to the enchantment and the fanatical compulsions of this type of festival, you just go through life in bemused addiction and that's that. Whatever one might think of the forbidding parochialists who wield the all-Welsh rule like a tomahawk and grin as they point at the number of lacerated scalps they've left in the valleys of Glamorgan and Monmouthshire, this still remains the most fascinating and cordial cultural phenomenon on earth.

Yes, despite all the curious suggestion of vestry intrigue, the proudly vaunted inadequacy of the catering (no beer tent), it still wears the old slogan: '*Calon wrth galon*' like a crown. That motto, 'Heart with Heart'— to be seen on the ancient Eisteddfod chair of Powys—still puts its finger on the enduring appeal of this great tribal conjunction of song, verse, craft, hiraeth and gossip.

That is one thing about a small nation which is capable of such a relatively vast concourse of its artistically active citizens; the whole social, domestic anatomy of the land can be gone over inch by inch. At intervals in the glorious volleys of vocalism and bardry, the sly, twisting mouths of an eloquent and witty people pool the diverting aberrations of every hamlet from Anglesey to Aberthaw. At the end of Eisteddfod week a bard has been crowned and a million closets aired.

If a layman is dismayed by what he might think an astonishing preponderance of ministers of religion in the crowds that ambulate between the marquees and booths, then he must remember that for a couple of centuries the chapel has been a characteristic part of our idiom, and that no nation has come nearer to being a theocracy, a people in vassalage to its preachers. It is part of the protective restraint of a people naturally

over-passionate. In Scotland, in ancient times, the pagan rapture in-
herent in most poets and most poetry was given its head, and the
authorities were driven to classing the bards of their land as 'a class of
frenzied vagabonds'. Not so in Wales; take a look at the Gorsedd mem-
bers as they shuffle to the crowning. An impeccably tidy lot. All passion,
if not spent, tightly on the lead.

The great dynasty of preachers shaped our soul and established the
rules of our not inconsiderable rhetoric. And behind the preacher has
always stood the image of the powerfully literate ploughman and miner
who have given to our working people an impressive and articulate
dignity. That is why the Eisteddfod cuts so deep into our social earth.
There is not a single artist in Wales today who, in his earliest years, was
not made more aware and communicative by the cult of self-expression
developed by the teeming vestries of our valleys. That is why, in certain
phases of the Eisteddfod, one detects a certain yearning for a return to
the chapel's day of dominance. Behind it there is a good deal of historic
justice.

There are few Welshmen over the age of thirty-five whose childhood
was not a shell-burst of eisteddfodic activity, sparked off by the great
legion of musical *aficionados* who supervised our Sunday schools. Each
and every one of us, from the time he got the shawl out of his mouth and
could shout '*Yma!*' ('Here!') when the Eisteddfod conductor called out
the name under which he had entered, was an Eisteddfodwr, a real gone
guy behind the banner of the festival.

In the earliest Penny Readings our artistic limbs were massaged for a
lifetime of cultural jousting and tuft-hunting. The training was Spartan
and you had to be pretty sharp to hold your own around the vestry bends.
In a tiny way I did fairly well as a prizewinner. I must, in my best
stretches, have been one of the few really healthy units in the economic
life of my part of the Rhondda.

The adjudicators in our small contests were nearly always the same;
two very pensive deacons judging the recitations and two voters of a
more Bohemian sort on the singing. One of the recitation judges was a
man of stern and anti-democratic bent, convinced that humanity would
blow its top and go off on some long, gross Saturday night of miscel-
laneous debauchery if ever released from its great restraining trusses of
dogma and intimidation. His face always lit up when I bounded up the
pulpit steps and made the tiles bounce with a rendering of Coriolanus's
famous skin-stripping assessment of the plebs. I also had a piece from the
Book of Job that made him purr like a cat in cream.

27

Bards and the Druid Circle

These were legitimate tactics. In the Eisteddfod world a close study of the temperament and taste of the adjudicator was as important as the timbre of voice or the dramatic angle at which one held one's sheet music. At those same Penny Readings one of the vocal adjudicators was a man of desperately sentimental sadness. He had been washed up on more or less permanent duty at the Penny Readings after the bumpiest emotional life since Hosea, whom he often quoted. A dozen jiltings and a certain jocose liking for being looted by every girl he met, made him an easy target for the sadder, soggier type of lyric.

If at the beginning of the bouts I saw his mood was particularly shadowed, I would choose with care from my quiver of deathbed chants and quick-action mid-Victorian weepies. 'We'll kiss away our tears when we cross the Great Divide', or one of the most neurasthenic songs ever written and which never failed to send my father racing for the ear-plugs and a shillelagh, 'Do not dally on hearing the call, In the grave is an answer to all.'

When my rivals saw the tears gather in the adjudicator's eye, and watched him roll his head in helpless abandon under the downpour of suggested sorrow, they would stuff their copies back in their pockets and wonder if it would be too grave an infringement of vestry-law if they arranged to have me jumped and sandbagged in the shadows of the porch on the following Tuesday.

The prizes at these early and radiant Eisteddfods were not lavish, but they struck us as having the splendour of the chairs now made with deep and loving craft for the winning bards at the National Eisteddfods. They were small satin bags attached to ribbons that went around the neck, and it was the convention to wear these articles rather like a mayor's chain on the way home, showing off and tempting footpads, for in the bag would be a threepenny or sixpenny bit.

By the time puberty came along and loosened the tight grip I had had on the Penny Readings for many years, I had won so many of these satin bags they had furnished the fabric to provide fancy blouses for the whole front row of a dance band organised by one of my brothers and called The Gitanos, an outfit which, under the protective tactic of looking frenzied and exotic, managed to work off a record number of wrong notes on to the public. The threepences and sixpences, which might have meant my beginning as a tycoon, I spent on so much toffee I was denounced by a senior deacon as licentious and a potential diabetic.

The excitement of leaving the valley for a major Eisteddfod in some adjoining *cwm* was unforgettable. For young male reciters dark velvet

trousers seemed to be regarded as a kind of obligatory court wear, and indeed they seemed to bring a fine sensual edge to certain vowels. This could lead to tense moments, for a bit of traditional chicane was to keep entering a boy for an age-group that he had long left. One often saw a boy, heavily adolescent, wearing velvet trousers that had been a fair fit when he had worn them for the under-ten competition. And when we were marshalled outside the bus his mother would be on hand to see that this youth had the seat by the driver with plenty of leg room so that he would not subject the fabric to too many stresses. The boy had also been instructed to keep his gestures on the stage to a minimum and to make his whole posture as recessive as possible.

For the mothers generally the Eisteddfod meant days of painful solicitude. I remember being in a bus bound for Maesteg, then, as now, an eisteddfodic hub. I was tidily dressed, in a dark sort of way, for I had been entered to compete under the *nom de chant* of Janus in the Junior Open Solo to sing a piece called 'The Promised Land', a defeatist lyric, strongly in favour of the grave, against the drink and scored for a deep, plangent alto.

I was champing at a very crumbly type of cracker. This had been recommended to me as a means of relaxing pre-Eisteddfod nerves by my teacher, a keen competitor himself. He had never won any prizes but he could carry a waistcoatful of cracker crumbs with more aplomb than any man I have seen. I was leaning forward talking to a friend in the seat in front, when a mother's hand grasped my wrist. 'Stop that,' she said. 'You are dropping those crumbs deliberately down our Meirion's neck. You know he's ticklish, our Meirion. You know he never sings his best when he's itching on the stage.'

Minor eisteddfods are commonly held in marquees. The 'National' of course exists mainly in the vast pavilion which makes its way annually north and south, inflated for the great week and then deflated for its eleven months' rest, like a massive lung, which is just what it is.

I can recall some very picturesque marquees. They could add a lot of tension to the event. Often erected in too great haste by amateurs they could be notoriously fissile. In a high wind one could be torpedoed right off the stage by a loose flap. One often saw members of a male voice group, lashed back from a dozen cosy hostelries by devout and dour committee men, chundering around the marquee looking for the correct entrance and sent hurtling by the innumerable guy-ropes and asking the conductor, when at last they formed their crescent on the stage, for five minutes' grace for the removal of clods.

31

I was once a member of a group entered in a mid-Glamorgan eisteddfod for the Action Song for the Under Twelves. The song was 'Ye Mariners of England'. We had been fitted out by our families with what they thought a rough version of naval uniform. This rig, as you would expect from so essentially landlocked an area as Porth, was inaccurate, and our gestures as we did an impression of a rapid horn-pipe brought many frowns from the more Calvinistic adjudicators.

It had rained for days. The canvas flap above the stage bulged and darkened with water in a fashion that brought offers from the Liverpool council. On our last thundering note the flap burst and we took rank as the first action-song team to stick together as a group while being actively washed through the main entrance of the marquee. One adjudicator gave us extra points for realism, but he was dripping and giddy with shock at the time.

These are scraps of recollection, but multiplied a million times they explain the wonderful glow of that first week in August when the Gorsedd trumpeters bring the National Eisteddfod once again to life. No faction fight between the Welsh-speaking folk of Wales and those from whom the language has been taken can impair the toughness of this festival. It has ridden bravely on some of the highest and most treacherous waves of national mischance. It was at a time of intense doubt, danger and division that the bards and the following multitudes came together to hold the first Eisteddfod. The Romans were departing from Britain. The void they left was full of howlings from the bitter east. To say the good word for warmth, hope and harmony, the newly elected chief of the Welsh, the man with the curious cocktail of a name, Owain ap Maxen Wledig, convened the first great tribal salutation to art and peace.

The present period is also one of doubt and division. The splendid emotional and intellectual qualities that go to make up Welshness are likely to be dissipated in a squalid dispute about the sounds clacked by the tongue to express ideas. You might be pleasing the bones of Hywel Dda by writing 'cwcw' instead of 'cuckoo' but there are many of us who do not see that it matters greatly.

And time, which erodes beaches, faces, faiths, will do as much for even so venerable a language as the Welsh. As the hierarchy of the new industries linked intimately with London, ousts the old dominance of the manse in our Establishment, the glow will die away from behind the neo-chauvinists. Simple electronics will do the rest. The most banal of television culture will break the back of the most vigorous village culture. Out of the gloom comes Merlin urging a more tolerant assessment by the

Gorsedd Circle of the need to keep the non-Welsh-speaking Celts within the racial fold.

*   *   *

I do not know who invented beer but I can say right off who have made the most fuss about it: the Welsh. No nation can ever have bred such a covey of drought-fanciers, people who can identify a glass of beer with the last emblem of evil. In the autumn of 1961 their drums were beating louder from Bettws-y-Coed to Raglan, Aberystwyth to Abersychan, rallying the prim and self-denying for their last stand in defence of the traditional gaunt Welsh Sabbath, the day on which we padlock the taverns and send malt, as outlawed as R. Hood, to do the best it can in the maquis. Battlements of bowlers and Asquith collars are looming out of the strange, dark social terrors which inspired the most fanatical temperance associations.

The most raffish Celt is bound to have in his bones a kind of respect for these people. They permeated every moral cranny of our childhood. Through the Band of Hope we were the objects of mass recruitment into the anti-liquor phalanx. I took a pledge to renounce wine and beer, with a codicil to be cautious even with cocoa, at the age of seven and eight. At nine I turned up to the rehearsal of a vestry cantata with my breath faintly tainted by the smell of some innocent herb-beer. I was hauled out and made to repeat the pledge in a ringing voice. Part of the rehearsal time was spent in instructing the other children in the art of how most cuttingly to shrink away from me. On the social front I had a lonely time: on the emotional front I did better. I was the nearest the local girls had come to meeting a rake at vestry-level.

I learned so many songs in praise of water it is a wonder I have not since been spotted and called up as a promotional agent by those people who want to sell our rain to the Midland cities. I would sing these songs to my father who, as a lover of ale, lagged only a noggin or two behind the great soak of Welsh mythology, Seithenyn the Arrant Drunkard. In a looser social context he would have sold me to the gypsies. One of my chirpier numbers contained these lines:

> A greater delight life never will bring
> Than the touch of my lips on a crystalline spring.
> Wine I renounce, and lust, its daughter,
> For the simple grace of a glass of water.

The final pellet as far as my father was concerned came when I became the assistant to a temperance lecturer. At ten years of age I was a premier battler against drink, and had been given, as a prize by a regional association, a novel called *The Awakening of Waldo Wilkins*, for the clarity of my songs about water. This Wilkins was a drunkard who had sent two brewers to the Lords and cast a pall over his particular valley. I forget the events that hoisted him out of his torpor and on to the wagon, but I needled my father by calling him Wilkins. As a result of this award the lecturer allowed me to carry parts of his equipment, screen and slides, to illustrate his exposure of rotgut.

I persuaded my father that his life would rush straight into crisis if he did not take a long, clear look at these slides. My father, in return for a promise that I would stop putting the knock on hops in the house itself, came along and spent an hour with his eyes popping and his hands clenched on a vestry bench. The slides showed pictures of different men in progressive phases of alcoholic delirium, an exhaustive catalogue of insane depravity. They all looked like stills from a Lon Chaney film called *The Penalty*, in which Chaney goes mad as the result of mutilation. There were also slides that claimed to be microscopic studies of ale, showing it to be charged with perilous organisms of the octopus type. They must have been submarine shots of a weed-choked moat, possibly the one at Caerphilly, near which town the lecturer lived, for he was the sort of man who would have gone under any sort of water to put beer in a bad light.

My father put a stop to this phase of my life with a few crude counter-measures. He wrote a letter to the local paper saying that if there were creatures roaming about in ale similar to the ones he had seen on the slides, then he personally would have wound up as a brief snack years before. Then he persuaded a friend of his, a converted toper called Pym, with a huge baritone voice that had flattened two Eisteddfod tents, and demented three adjudicators who had crept up too close to Pym to see if they could identify the song he was supposed to be singing, and who found their tympanum coming away in their hands.

My father gave Pym his orders and I would find this mammoth way-laying me every whipstitch and shouting right at me, 'Look not on the wine when it is red.' Then he would drag me to a crystalline spring on the hillside at the foot of the hill behind our house, telling me that he had heard from my father that I liked nothing better than to place my lips on the surface of the freshet. I don't know whether Pym was working to an agreed brief or just didn't know his own strength, but when I found the spring lapping the back of my neck my view of water changed utterly.

This phobia has a considerable root in history. Welsh society has been scalloped by some pretty considerable deprivations. Among her farmers one sees nothing of that jocund and ruddy satisfaction apparent in the snugs around a Cotswold square on market day. Marsh and stone between them have dictated a broad patch of grim husbandry in which the sharper type of goat has been known to threaten to sue the farmer. The quarrymen of the north often seem to subsist in a kind of desperation which has exactly the colour and quality of the slate they slice. The residual incident in their fiction appears to be the courtship of an ageing couple who have a two-day honeymoon in oilskins during the monsoon at Dinas Mawddwy.

In the south there was a scalding haste in the diffusion of pits. The endless chains of tiny houses, so small even the mice had to join in the singing, bred in many an itching desire to be elsewhere. Safety measures in the mines were so slap-happy that methane explosions crept into our inherently musical society as a kind of percussion section. The mining villages were spun around our gulches like the webs of an insensitive spider. The chapels throbbed with hymns of apocalyptic yearning, and the sermons spoke with authority of doom, and shot down any hint of relaxed sensuality as if it were a raving dog. They were the listening posts of an eternal terror and forbidding, a placing of sentinels on the grey edge of an arctic night. People older than myself claim to have found in them great effusions of love and joy, but I must have been standing at the wrong angle. Every young deacon in the locality seemed to sharpen his teeth on me, to be dedicated to catching me in some posture that would expose me as a hell-bent elf. I grew up sour on the black-serge boys.

Against this background it is easy to understand why the pubs developed into troughs, places of a discomfort that would appal a Bedouin, where to be entertained took second place to being stupefied, and where ten or fifteen pints at one session would bring all the resentments of an indefensible environment blackly and swiftly to the boil. Between the two poles of howling revivalism and militant besottedness there was little free and gracious territory.

One can often hear elderly miners say of their early years: 'I didn't particularly want the chapel; I didn't particularly want the pub, because I felt that both were ignoring some valuable part of the whole human statement. So I tried a bit of theosophy, and, when that made no sense, I took up pigeon-fancying. Dull lot, those pigeons. I tried to cure them of the homing instinct. I tried to make them roam the earth and test the flavour of many lands as I would have liked to do if I hadn't been tied to a

Places of Discomfort

low seam and a tall wife, but they had been flattered by Darwin, who had done research into the ways of these birds, and they kept coming back.'

Many of the people who are still hostile to the 1961 Licensing Bill as if it were a fresh round of vandalism and rape, will have had their imaginations nourished on the kind of thing that happened every Saturday night in my village. At stop-tap the legion of drinkers from the many pubs would fall into step on the steep road leading to the top terraces. For a short interval there would be some singing and discussion with a simmer of violence just beneath. Then a shout of disagreement. The subject could be theology, politics, music; the merits of total over pedal baptism, the sincerity of Lloyd George and the point of long hair; the flatness of tone of some local choir-leader. Any one of these topics could fire the rick and in an instant two hundred fists and half as many flagons would be swinging. Had they fought progressively north or south and vanished out of earshot it could have been tolerated. But the compact mass just swung back and fore in the main street. It had the grim rhythm of the Somme Salient.

Even funerals could be made the vehicle for some fair bouts of debauch. Especially funerals held in the graveyards of villages sequestered in the middle of the broad plateaux that divided the valleys. Coffins had to be man-handled up goat tracks, and were more than once mislaid by the panting mourners. The service at the village was loud and long, a field-day for a booming compassion, with each fresh hymn-chorus coming out in a thicker jacket of velvet. And when grief had had its say wassail of a classic sort would be declared. It was a great uproarious vote of censure on death and muscular strain.

The local option clause in the Licensing Bill caused a few snorts of dismay. It's bad enough, said the pro-beer boys, to find money for drinking. It's too tough when one needs a map and transport as well. It revived memories of the 'bona-fide' drinking of yesteryear. To have a drink on Sunday one had to prove that one was a 'bona-fide' traveller, that one had come a sufficient distance to qualify for irrigation. Sympathetic landlords would place outside their doors boxes of dust which clients could sprinkle on to their shoes to suggest a long trek on a waterless road. This dust caused the Welsh lung a fair amount of trouble. The temperance faction opposed the local option on the grounds that drunken sinners would go roaring back to their dry areas in lethal vehicles. If as much energy went into drink and sex as their enemies make out we would be a more interesting species.

There is no doubt that when Sunday opening came to Wales there should have been a move to commemorate, with some special emblem of affection, those pubs that stand along the English border which were the first to meet the eyes of the anti-Sabbatarians in their coaches and cars as they rolled eastward to anoint their tormented glottis with malt. The end of restriction has brought to a close a whole culture of stealth. There have been pubs which, through all the decades of prohibition, have provided a marginal refreshment for people who have no wish to belong to a club: 'Give three soft knocks and say you know the ex-Archdruid.'

I heard a significant story about this type of tavern. A licensee from Yorkshire had come to stay with his wife's people in a mining village in Monmouthshire. He liked a Sunday morning gill and loathed going into a club for it. He was told not to worry. There was a pub to which Sunday access was easy. On the Sunday morning he found himself making his way to the pub with a small cloud of conspirators around him. They filtered into the backyard from a network of back-lanes.

Inside the pub they took their places around the big smoke-room. They had to keep silent in case some agent of the pious might be perambulating on the pavement outside. The bar was cut off by a heavy iron grill behind which one could dimly see the landlord. Our friend said it was like visiting a member of the Mafia in gaol. Then somebody shouted, 'Now!' and the grill was thrown up. Everybody in the room queued up and got a drink at lightning speed and the grill crashed down again. The convention of standing rounds was suspended in the urgency of defying the Sabbath. If you were in the room you bought yourself a drink, regardless. The opening of the grill was a commandment. Our friend had barely taken two gulps before the cry rang out again, 'Now,' and up shot the grill once more, and the clients rushed forward in another lemming act. By one o'clock the Yorkshireman was out for the count, and the landlord was going up and down with the grill.

It has been interesting to see how the adjustment to today's more limber arrangements has been made. In the past one excess begat another. The wrinkles are out of our bellies; the light has immeasurably improved; we speak more softly one to the other. Whiffs of urbanity are reaching even the most intolerant bigot, and even the most soused of hellions is beginning to turn away from squalor as we once learned to turn away from leprosy. And once the pubs have freed themselves from the charge of being outposts of the devil, places where customers expected to endure a purgatorial discomfort, perhaps the average Welsh licensee might overcome his addiction to wooden benches and kitchen chairs and provide us with some civilised seating.

3 Revivalism and the Falling Larks

NORMALLY, in Meadow Prospect, there is a cool obliquity in the approach to sexual friendships. The mood of caution is so generally established that ardour is kept on a wire-rope leash. But even so, we once came near to a Romeo and Juliet story.

We have a large, handsome statue in the north-west corner of the cemetery to prove it. It is the likeness in stone of a splendid, full-mouthed young woman, and on the pedestal are the words: 'Jennie Bell, Who Sang.' Her mouth, speaking from an unfaded memory of Jennie, was too heavy, but that was a consistent fault in the work of the monumental mason who sculpted it. His name was Mervyn Buckley and his work on women's heads was always defiantly a censure of his wife, a thin-lipped, life-whittling woman with whom Buckley had never truly been at ease.

The Romeo to Jennie Bell's Juliet was a quiet, chronically considerate man called Penry Murdoch. They exchanged only a few words and not a single kiss. They made free contributions of themselves to love, were consumed utterly by it, and their final reward must be the absolute minimum recorded even in the calamitous annals of this tricky impulse.

Penry Murdoch was a banksman; that is, he operated the machinery which worked the cage that took the men up and down the shaft of the colliery at which he worked. In all things else he was wretchedly shy, but left alone with the levers and wheels that filled his little shed, he had all the confidence and gaiety of fulfilled genius.

The men said that never had they been taken to the bottom or brought to the top with such velvet perfection. The men had memories of banksmen so rough and flippant in their traffic with the winding gear they brought them hurtling down to the pit-bottom at a speed that left their teeth half-way down the shaft, and brought them back to the surface in a rocketing flight that had caused many of them to walk home

Rhondda Impression

with their boots still in the cage. There were some very dour Sandemanians among those old winders who were influenced by their basic pro-death point of view to feel that once man had been lured by sin into a fine, deep hole, it was a silly concession to the soft, sensual side of our make-up to haul him up again. So, nightly, the men, who did the trip into and out of the light guided by Penry Murdoch, drank thanks to Penry's sure, compassionate fingers.

Then Penry, in his middle forties, fell in love with Jennie Bell, a girl less than half his age, as often happens with these silent, dedicated artists. For he was certainly an artist. His art was to take the terror out of that dirty, hurtling trap in the old Tuberville mine. And anyone who can take the terror out of anything, out of religion, table manners, toothache, love that comes too early or too dumb, anything, that man has a symphony to his credit.

The family of Jennie Bell lived in a row of tiny cottages alongside the river. It was called Lilac Lane, but the river at that sluggish bend made a heavy smell that mocked the name of the cottages. The cottages are not there any more. They were so damp that the slates, under a less rigid rent system, would have floated off. The flood of 1929 came up to the bed-room floor. So, after taking the tenants off by boat, they decided to tear the place down. I was sorry to see it go because I could never pass the place without seeing the face of Jennie Bell again and hearing her voice. Even in a zone as melodious as this her voice had the sure seal of great-ness on it. You've heard Ponselle and Tebaldi. That kind of warmed silk.

The Bell family lived in the middle house of Lilac Lane, the dampest of the lot. The surrounding houses used to squeeze their surplus over the Bells. Naboth Bell, the father, was an inept, philogenetic man. He had the look of a worried merman, as if he knew that he should be elsewhere and never would be. The whole family was tubercular, as whole families often were in those days. You would see entire groups of children vanish into thin air or thick earth. It was as if there were a zone of autumn waiting for them when they got to thirteen, fourteen, and they'd go quietly, like leaves.

We had preachers who had worked out such superb, sure-fire sermons to be given at the gravesides of the young they would have sued anyone who came along with a quick cure for chest ailments. The leap and slash of socially nourished disease has always been one of the great gushers of popular poetry. Being lyrical about young death became one of the deadliest hobbies of the region. That is what kept so many people lost. Tears play hell with the eyesight.

Seven of the Bell family went that way. Maturity would only have to rest on them for about six months and off they'd go, scurrying like mice into the easy dark.

Jennie was the youngest and the only one to survive out of her teens. She was very beautiful. She had a kind of defiant brightness about her, as if daring the fingers that had not yet closed around her throat to do their worst. And I've never again heard a voice like hers in all my life. Just as if she was trying to say something on behalf of all the brothers and sisters who had never managed to make an impress.

It was with her that Penry Murdoch fell in love. And he did it in exactly the same sort of way as he handled the cage at work. Softly, and with a dread of mishaps. He never said a word to her. He was helped in this by Naboth Bell. His attachment to the girl was fanatical, riveted to her all the more securely by the deaths of the other children. He had been told that passion and marriage would bustle a physical type like Jennie into the tomb. The need to tend and give this voice to the world became an obsession with him. It was as if he knew that in the oyster of his great and many troubles the rub of absurdity had finally fashioned a pearl.

He was told stories by the song fanciers of the town, of great divas having been kept alive within a breath of death by the devotion of their parents. And Naboth brought his devotion to a peak of fitness. Any lover seen approaching Lilac Lane was likely to be received by Bell's boot. A lot of innocent parties, well out of touch with love and who might never have heard of Jennie Bell, elements like insurance agents and political canvassers trying to tickle people forth from under their rocks, got the shock of their lives when half-way through a sentence they got the full force of Bell's toe-cap, and a lot of rhetoric thrown in branding them as ravishers.

If a watch-dog was what Jennie needed, she would have been alive to this day. The old man restricted her singing, too. He didn't want to waste the beauty of it on Lilac Lane. He was convinced that one day a man would come, a man of power and discernment and charm, who would stop and listen. Then he would take Jennie racing through all the lush and lighted places of the world. A man came all right.

In the summer of 1927 the revivalist, Raglan Redrup, came to Meadow Prospect. You may not have heard Raglan's name because he did most of his preaching in Canada. He was a handsome man and it was said that at one time he had platoons of converts whirling around him like a tattoo. His marching song, 'Rise now, rise now with Raglan,

Ye stricken sinners, rise', had left many of the peccant too hoarse for serious impiety.

When he came to Meadow Prospect he put on a good air, but things were far from well with him. In age he would have been a little under forty but he looked more. His hair had become quite grey and his face had deep wrinkles in which he had trained the shadows to appear almost articulate. He had anguish on a lead like a performing dog.

He had been on the highest plane of evangelism since the age of eighteen, and that is a wearing thing. He was short of funds. He had invested a lot of money in a gold-boom town of the American west. The gold seemed to have seen Raglan coming because it withdrew like magic as soon as Raglan had paid the last deposit on his shares, and was really coming to enjoy the flavour of cigars. He formed an association with a widow of agnostic views. She was wealthy. Raglan, after the lambasting he had taken on the market and the sapping fervour of twenty long revivalist tours, was in a mood for some cool, even negative notions about God.

He urged the widow to channel some of her money into bodies that were out to denounce gold and fundamentalism. Raglan looked forward to an old age of pleasant doubt and irremovable affluence. But the relatives of the widow's late husband got active. They were canny pietists and quick-footed when making for coin. They sued the widow right and left and proved her irresponsible before a pre-Darwinian judge. They stripped her of everything she had.

Raglan left the widow and came back to Meadow Prospect in a last lap of desperation. For him it must have been something like the end of the road. He was tired. He had lost the vivid fervour that had once given his face the radiance of noon, and his larynx the resonance and toughness of an anvil. He had always been one of the loudest preachers, and one of the reasons for his having gone to Canada was a suggestion that there he might have more room to let the echoes spread.

The Meadow Prospect Free Church Council seemed from the start to have a fierce down on Raglan. They had been told that Raglan had been seen and heard in pubs sardonically mocking other revivalists and denouncing them as scruffy shamans. They refused him the use of any of the larger chapels.

Raglan got hold of a large tent from somewhere and pitched it in that patch of marshland between Lilac Lane and the main body of the town. The place has been drained now but at that time the people of Lilac Lane had a dark river in front and a fever zone at the back. It was as treacherous a piece of bog as you can imagine, and it shows what a desperate stage Raglan must have reached to go there at all without being able to offer his followers a lifebelt with every hymnal. He seemed to be assembling the pieces for some black climax. He was down to the last stitch of weariness, and with thoughts of the widow, no doubt, whistling around the bare walls of his brain like the saddest of birds.

He got his tent delivered, the ancient canvas ravelling in the hands of the unwrappers. I was working at the time with a small firm of contractors to whom Raglan had come for the furnishing of his marquee. One of my employers was a lay preacher who had been rebuffed by the Church Council. Being eloquent and in the timber trade he had come to fancy himself as a kind of Noah, and he had developed a way of hammering suggestively at the woodwork of the chapels in which he preached, putting the sectaries on edge, for Meadow Prospect is squarely in the middle of the rain belt.

So my employer was prepared to help Raglan. Even so, by the time Raglan had fitted himself up with a reasonable pulpit, and there are certain rigorous minima in the design of these fitments if one is to keep morally ahead of the audience, he was obviously at the bottom of his pocket. He could not afford many seats and only a handful of duckboards for the floor. You could see the heavier voters getting shorter as they went into the marsh. You may not have seen this happen but it does not help a preacher. Physically it was the greatest challenge any revivalist has had to face and Raglan was in no mood to face it. You can enjoy tragedy if you're fit for it, but after all those disappointments with the gold and the widow, and his larynx going on the National Health, it was too much for Raglan.

On the second night of the mission the audience was a lot smaller than it had been for the first night. I had to be there because my firm wanted to be sure that the furniture that Raglan was hiring stayed in sight and was reasonably dry. Also there was a forecast of high winds and I was under orders to keep a hold on the canvas of the marquee every time the wind started to sound louder than Raglan.

Raglan was in poor spirits and he was not helped by the sight of me giving a helpful jerk to the odd voter whose duckboard looked like going under. And the smell of that marsh was enough to cancel out every good belief mankind has ever had about itself.

Five minutes after Raglan began talking, Jennie Bell came into the tent. Raglan had his head disconsolately down and did not notice her. But I did. As soon as I saw her the whole air of the tent lightened, and I stared like a dog at the bewitching pallor of her cheekbones, the immense power and pity of her deep, dark eyes. I rushed to get a chair for her and the smile she gave me when she accepted it made me feel that I could have laid my body down on that marsh to keep any tiny part of her body dry.

Then Raglan saw her. For a whole minute he fell quite still and silent. He looked at her with the same entranced astonishment as I had felt. Then he flung his head back in a kind of ecstasy of despair and started again.

He tried to whip himself into a state of rhetorical heat. But his words and feelings were on too rough a road. The damp air had got into his lungs and the audience were a primely chilling crew. And one of the chilliest of the lot was Jennie Bell's father who had just come into the tent and was nudging her to come away. Whatever noon arose at the sight of Jennie went promptly down at the sight of her father. If you got near enough to him you winced at the unique grip that life had perfected on him.

I moved closer to Raglan to watch his face. The little steam of pleasure I had seen in it at the entrance of Jennie Bell had quite gone now. His thoughts were distant and winged with the blackest disgust and regret. I could see the memory of America and the widow rising in Raglan, the thought of deep, bodily comfort, security and the urbane delightful indifference to the grimaces of the soul.

I was dodging around a little pool that had formed in one of the corners of the marquee when I caught his eye. He had opened his mouth for some mechanical invocation of grace. Then he closed it tight with a gasp of dismay. It was clear that he was now ready to lapse into a climactic silence in which, as far as he was concerned, the audience could go home and the tent fall down.

Then Jennie Bell started to sing. She just stood up and started to sing. The sound of it went clear around the marquee like a belt of explosive warmth. I suppose I was about the only person who was not wholly surprised. There had been a great pity on her face as she stared up at Raglan. At first I had thought it was just the worried expression that people in a marsh and expecting a big revelation often wear. But I had looked closer and it was first-rate pity without a doubt. It had grown richer as she had taken in the details of Raglan's crisis of terrified sorrow. It had taken hold of her body, her throat. And up she got, to sing.

Her father tried to lead her away. 'Come on, Jennie, don't grieve me, Jennie,' he kept muttering and he frowned down at the damp earth.

But there was a serene obstinacy on her face as she gestured him away. And in the pause between the recitative and the aria of the item she was singing I heard her saying quite clearly to her father, 'Dad, you can go and jump in the Dusky.' The Dusky was the name of the river that flowed past Lilac Lane.

It was as if she alone had been able to see down the dark shaft at the bottom of which Raglan was preparing to curl up. With her very first note, a crowner with her full chest behind it, she commanded him back to life. What she sang was, 'Hear Me, Israel'. Until that night I had always considered it a gift from God to the rowdier and more bullying type of soprano. I had always thought it too heavy an item for such a frail girl as Jennie Bell. But she sang it that night with a supernatural force and joy that gave the dripping air of that tent the warmth of the tropics.

Raglan came down from the pulpit. He took her hand and led her up. She was still singing at full tilt when he came and stood behind her on the pulpit, smiling and touching her lightly and encouragingly on the shoulder. At his urging she sang every song she knew. She knew a lot of songs. At the end of each item Raglan would close his eyes, lift his arm and say, 'The Lord has just sung through the mouth of Jennie Bell. The Lord and Jennie Bell will now sing . . .'

And he would lean over and get the name of the next song from Jennie who had it ready on her lips as if she had been training for just this moment all her life.

At the meeting's end, as Raglan was escorting Jennie to the tent's entrance, her father grabbed her away from him.

'I'll be back tomorrow night,' she shouted as her father hurried her through the darkness towards Lilac Lane.

And the next night she was back. The tent was packed. Volunteers brought benches and duckboards. For a clear two years people in Meadow Prospect had been feeling the need for a miracle, and Jennie plucking Raglan from the ashes qualified as that.

Raglan had Jennie by his side in the pulpit. He enveloped her from the start with the sort of passion that must go into most murders. He confined himself to a mere soft-voiced pointing of mood. And then he would release Jennie's voice like an enchantment. He bought her a long, snow-white dress and by the end of the mission's first week her face was whiter even than the dress.

When she came into the marquee we could see that she was leaning heavily against Raglan's body as they advanced up the central aisle towards the pulpit. But part of that might have been simple affection, for you could tell from the way she looked at him that he was in and out of all her dreams.

Singing is a thing that tires. But singing with the nerves bristling for the first assault of love, that's a chiller. Ten of the best baritones I know in the zone lost vocal pace because they had lust camped between their arias. And then there was the air in that marquee. We know the trouble canaries get with methane.

Jennie's parents tried to plead with Raglan, telling him of the way in which their other children had died. They told him of their fears that the strain of all this singing in a marsh might do great harm to Jennie. But Raglan had his answer. He told them the responsibility was scarcely his. It was God who had directed Jennie to open her mouth to start her first song at that very moment when Raglan had been about to hurl his mission to the devil. And the same God would see Jennie strong enough to bear the mission of her snow-white heart throughout the land. 'Snow-white heart.' That is what he said. That is exactly what he said to Jennie's father and mother. I was there. I was bringing a fresh batch of benches into the marquee because the mission was now booming.

Jennie's father just looked at Raglan and said very softly, that there are so many men who are soap factories in themselves it almost made one feel sorry for the future of dirt. It was the only time I had ever heard Mr Bell come out with a long, thoughtful sentence, with a hint of subversion in it. But the circumstances were exceptional.

Her parents, guided by some people who were against Raglan, tried locking Jennie in her room. But she leaned out of the upstairs window and told them in the calmest voice you ever heard, that if they did not stop this nonsense she or God would come down and kill them.

They believed her. It was the kind of statement that does not sound out of place in areas like Lilac Lane. I saw all this because Raglan had sent me to the house in Lilac Lane with some old-fashioned salves that Jennie was to gargle and rub in for her throat. He said he had got these cures from an old prospector in Canada who had scoured the Rockies for the right herbs, and had slept rough for thirty years without a single sneeze on account of the stuff he distilled from these simples. I did not see that the prospector had ever faced the same problems as Jennie Bell, but it was not my job to make things more confused. So I said nothing.

But this reliance of Raglan on secular agencies worried me. When I went back early that night to the tent he was there, alone. He was groaning and running his hands through his hair. He was in a sweat of anxiety and tramping about on the duckboards. I could see that in all sorts of ways he was beginning to get Jennie Bell on his conscience. I told him, in the quiet, jerky way of the young, that if he thought Jennie Bell was in need of salves the best thing he could do was to have some pity on the parents of Jennie who had already been slapped black and blue by mortality, and move on to the next town. I added, seeing that he was making no reply and causing the whole air of the tent to become unbearably tragic, that that prospector in Canada might have been abnormally strong and unable to sneeze even if he had wanted to. Just then Raglan turned up the volume of his groaning and I don't think he caught the last part of what I said.

Then he answered me. He told me to sit down on one of the benches so that I could take it all in, in calm. First, he told me that it was God's will. He said it mechanically, in a voice of sacking. He said it again, louder, and right into my face. Then he saw that working with those sub-contractors, a sub-human lot, had made me neutral in these matters. 'Jennie's destiny,' he said, 'has been revealed most plainly to me.' The quality of sacking had left his voice. It was now flat and sad in the way of most human voices.

Then he shouted right into the top of the marquee. 'I'm not afraid. I'm not afraid at all.'

'No, Mr Redrup.'

'Jennie and I will go on. I've never walked blind. I've always known where I'm going. I've accepted an invitation to preach with her in a large hall in the Midlands.'

'Oh, that's good, Mr Redrup.'

He made no answer to that. He just looked deaf and distant.

Then at that moment Jennie Bell herself walked into the tent. If the angel of death were already on her face, as it probably was, its wings were bright. She came towards where we were standing. Yards away from Raglan she raised her arms to embrace him. She did not seem to notice me. That quarrel with her parents had probably pushed her to a point where she could take in only one human being at one time. In a voice that was half-singing she said: 'I love you, Raglan Redrup.'

I tell you, there have been times when I have been hopeful about the future of sanity and the triumph of reason, and then I have recalled the face of Jennie Bell and her voice as she spoke those words, and I have become wisely cautious.

There was still an hour to go before the evening meeting began. Raglan dismissed me with a wave of his hand and he led Jennie into a hollow space beneath the platform of his pulpit. He had a kind of settee there on which he rested before starting to speak. Or has that settee sprouted from a dream somewhere in the years that have gone by since? I was young then and the thought of Jennie Bell has plunged a part of my mind into a hot sadness where all kinds of things might have grown.

When the meeting began Jennie was on the platform at Raglan's side. Previously she had followed the routine of that first night. At the end of Raglan's first great spurt she would stand up in the audience and start singing as she walked down the aisle in response to his beckoning hand. But that night she was on the platform from the start. Her dress was rumpled and shabby now, but no one would have noticed because she had a pallor that made it seem she was receiving guests for death. But her voice when she sang had a greater richness than ever before, as if her receding life had taken all its reserves into this one corner.

When I took a seat I found myself sitting next to Penry Murdoch. I got into quiet conversation with him because his chair happened to be on an especially soft part of the marsh. I got him the solid support of a duckboard I had taken from beneath the chairs of some stony, bigoted-looking voters it would have been a pleasure to see sinking out of sight.

Penry did not take his eyes off Jennie all night. The heat of his body was intolerable, and his back, as he clutched the seat in front of him, was agonisingly arched. Three times an usher came up to Penry and asked him if he was all right. That usher was tone-deaf and regarded Jennie's singing as a secular intrusion. Between the verbal contributions by Raglan he just walked about the marquee putting questions to people of the same sort as the one he had just put to Penry, making in this way a big reputation for Christian solicitude but not really expecting an answer, and just shaking his head sombrely and without hope when he got one.

On the way home that night Penry and I called in at the sawdust bar of a pub called The Easefull. Penry did not normally go into such places but that night he was in such a stupor of grief and longing he could have been led right across the Sahara without noticing the sand.

In the bar I noticed quite a number of men, all looking stooped, lame and disquieted, approach Penry and give him an accusing stare. Listening to some of the brusque, bitter remarks they made to Penry in between offers of a drink, I found that since Penry had started to burn for Jennie Bell his hand with the levers that worked the pit cage had gone to pot, and he had been hurtling these boys up and down the shaft at speeds that had rattled their reflexes to a standstill and caused them, on gaining the surface, to go over to the shed where Penry did his work and ask him what the hell he had against them now.

'His trouble is love,' I told these boys who had assembled around Penry in the bar of The Easefull. 'He is mad about that Jennie Bell who is now the hand-maiden and vocalist of Raglan Redrup, the missionary and evangelist, who is currently rekindling the faith in that marquee on the marsh. Penry has nothing against you boys and is probably quite ignorant that he is not giving you the same smooth ride as you've come to expect from him. It's just that he's in a daze of devotion for this Jennie Bell. He just doesn't know one end of the shaft from the other.'

They were all sympathetic and told Penry to do something about Raglan Redrup without delay while their spinal discs were still running in a roughly straight line from neck to beam. A few voters who muttered that a few pints a night would help Penry forget Jennie Bell altogether were told not to be negative.

'You've got to swoop down on that marquee, Penry,' said the spokesman of the majority group. 'You've got to rescue that girl from the tightening talons of that Redrup. And do it soon, because if you become any less serene in your handling of those levers in the winding shed, we are going to deepen that shaft by about ten feet, by sheer force of landing, unpaid.'

Penry thought about that advice for nearly a week. The crowds at the mission tent thickened, Raglan's oratory meanwhile grew thinner and more sporadic. He called on the magic of Jennie's singing more often. Raglan now held her hand as she sang, and even embraced her in a detached fatherly way when she came to the end of some more than ordinary song. The audience seemed to find something nourishing in the morbidity of this tableau. Raglan and Jennie wrapped the great applause around them, and found some refuge from the cold that was closing in on them both.

The rainy season had come again and the marsh was glad. I told Raglan that two of the duckboards had vanished from view but he did not seem to care. He said that as far as he was concerned the whole marquee could now go south beneath the bulrushes. 'I am fulfilled,' he said. I did not understand what he meant by this, and as he kept on saying it louder and louder I was glad to leave the marquee and report to my employers about the missing duckboards.

The following Saturday night when Jennie had sung twice the number of songs she normally did she collapsed. But she insisted on getting up and singing that very soothing old Sankey and Moody number, 'Flee as a Bird to your Fountain, Ye who are weary of sin.' A group of first-aid men and a passionate appeal from Raglan had brought her round, and she stood there looking like someone who has just slipped out of the tomb for a last glimpse. And her singing was lovelier than ever. Everyone was crying, some with that loud, almost joyful abandon that makes you wonder about the nature of some people's hungers.

As I walked home that night Penry Murdoch was at my side. I could feel a resolve hardening in him like a gallstone. He did not tell me what it was. But I could feel the resolve in him, and I could see the dark tightening of his small, kind face, and between that and the memory of Jennie's death-loaded eyes back there in the mission, I was glad to look up at the sky and let my mind slip into a blank, non-human context.

Penry's resolve was simple and drastic. He had gone along several times to The Easefull and the voters who assembled there had given him the gist of a hundred Voltairean tracts which dealt with the curious aims and effects of all such apocalyptic performers as Raglan Redrup. The boys in The Easefull, on top form at the prospect of a hard winter, convinced Penry that if he was going to strike a blow for Jennie Bell, he might just as well widen the scope of his mania and strike a blow for reason as well. So Penry's plan was to set a light to the marquee with Jennie, Raglan, and the audience all inside.

If he had asked me I could have told him that he would have been wasting his time. It would have taken a month's intensive drying and a hundred oxy-acetylene burners to have caused the slightest kindle in such a lavishly soaked article as that marquee.

Penry found himself a kerosene flare and approached the marquee in a big, slow semi-circle. He was seen by several people at a fair distance but he was taken by them to be some kind of clumsily built firefly that liked the neighbourhood of missionary tents on damp ground.

Penry worked his way in shakily from the periphery to start his work of igniting the canvas. He had a lot of trouble keeping his flare alight because it was a very inferior article, sold to him by some very perfidious voter who had a booth in Meadow Prospect market, and who had for a long time been using that particular flare only on that side of the booth where he kept his most ancient materials and did his shadiest deals. I suppose that Penry's plan was no more than to get the sectaries in a state of big panic when they found their zeal being laced with smoke, then nip in and rescue Jennie. I have often thought what a terrible situation that must have been for Penry, wandering about in that marsh. Feet wet,

arson jostling love for first place in his heart and trying to blow some continuous life into a third-rate flare.

Luck was not with Penry at all. On second thought it might have been. There is no way of judging things that are set against an essentially lunatic background. On the path through the marsh chosen by Penry a fissure had formed. From this fissure was issuing a record quantity of raw methane, marsh gas. The gas was just waiting for someone to come along with a naked flame. It was Penry. There was a small explosion. It tumbled Penry into the fissure and he died.

At the very moment of the bang Jennie Bell was on the very highest note of 'Hear Me, Israel'. The shock of the noise, the strain of the song and the collective jump of the audience did their work. She had another collapse and this time the first-aid men, although up on the platform like whippets and urged on by another passionate appeal from Raglan, were not enough.

She died on the platform. Raglan waved back the people who rushed forward. Alone he carried her down the aisle to the tent's entrance. It was a beautiful, compelling sight, for Raglan had just the face, head and shoulders for this type of absolute drama. No one paid any attention when a man rushed in and said that there had been an explosion out on the marsh, and that by the light of it the body of a man had been seen falling out of sight.

Jennie Bell had a fine funeral. Penry was buried on the same afternoon, but alongside the great weeping throng that turned out for Jennie his was a furtive affair. Just a few boys like those voters in The Easefull who shuffled through a neutral hymn and a prayer that all surviving colliery winders would take a lesson from the velvet touch that had been Penry's in the blessed days of his cool sanity.

Raglan Redrup took a keen interest in Penry and the way of his dying when I told him of Penry's hopeless love. He set up a company for the further exploitation of all the methane in the marsh. He did quite well. The first big thing he did out of the profits was to build that memorial to Jennie Bell on the north side of the Black Meadow. A young woman, with her head thrown back, singing.

4 The Way to the Sea

EVEN now the rattle of a train means just one thing to me. It is the bizarrely entranced day each summer when we valley children poured in our thousands down the sloping streets to the station, into the train, to edge out of the close, inclosing hills, through the lush fields of the Vale of Glamorgan, to the sea. At the first sight and sound of us the fish moved off a mile and kept a cold eye on the whole Sunday school movement that had sponsored our act of joy. Once a year, one magic glimpse of the sea.

On the day itself we paraded at dawn up and down the pavements, sniffing at the air, frowning at the formation of the clouds and daring them to put a damper on our delight. Usually they looked as if they had heard and were working hard at it. That valley was the saddest pocket in the whole dun suit of British weather.

But there will never be such optimists as those boys in the dawn weather patrol. The sky might look as if it were shaping up for the most baleful act of spleen since Noah, there might even be a cloudburst swilling the waiting trippers down to the bed of the Taff, we were not put off.

'It's all right. It's for heat. It's just a haze for heat. It's always the same. If you can't see the top of the mountain, watch out for sunstroke. Don't take coats. It'll be a scorcher. Just a handkerchief for the back of the neck stuffed into your cap and hanging loose like in the Legion.' Then we would limp home for a vapour rub and a stoup of hot broth. Our blood, after a broken night, tended to be thin and the early morning air, as a matter of principle in such an astonishing milieu, was mordant.

Active preparations began at seven. Any family taking less than a hundredweight of sandwiches was accused of trifling with the treat. We were the only tape-worms ever to appear publicly in blue serge.

57

Appetites were sharp even as we walked down to the vestry for our tickets.

'Hey, our Dad, could I have a sandwich? One of the roast porks?'

'Blod, Merf wants a roast pork.'

'At this time, a roast pork! The dearest and the best! All right then. But don't let him get at the fruit. He's a terror for the fruit. Last year we let him get at the bag at Porth. Bad in Ponty. Had to get off the train in Creigiau.'

The scene at the station was like a crisis in Babylon. Often a number of Sunday schools would go on the same day, at the same time. Then the local station master reached the heights of Job.

'No co-operation! No sympathy! No thought for the Great Western Railway. The biggest gathering of Christians since the revival of 1904, and all wanting to go to Barry on the same train. No love or trust among you. If one Sunday school went on its own it would be afraid the other four would be back home praying for heavy rain. There's that lot from Tregysgod. There's a crew. A rough lot, the last recruits to the faith before that Darwin put paid to innocence. If the train feels a bit low and bumpy when it pulls into Barry, those boys will have taken the wheels. Riffs! They should have gone by special camel at seven.'

On crowded days the slogan for each compartment was, 'Pack them in, there'll always be time to winkle you out of the woodwork at Barry.' It explains the superb breath-control of many Rhondda vocalists. On a really big treat they inhaled deeply at Penygraig and could not breathe out again until they got to Barry. It was a feeble child who could not get lost in that set-up.

'Where's Merfyn? Stop the train! Wave a flag! Is that him there with the jacket over his head? Look for him. Oh, there he is. Where was he, Enos?'

'Next compartment. Under that big soprano who tells fortunes. Madame Tetra Thomas. There she was sitting so jocose in the corner of the compartment, humming "Arise O Sun" as she always does at the beginning of a treat. Then she shouts to Mr Hallett, the guard, "This seat is very lumpy, Hallett." She gets up. There's our Merf. Crushed and blue.'

When the train swung west from Pontypridd our faces lost their defensive frowns and the sound of children singing spread from compartment to compartment. Children in the bottom layer of the rack were excused.

At Barry some shrewd lads, recalling the showers of pennies and oranges that kindly folk had dropped on them when they got lost the year before, made an instant bee-line for the Lost Children's Pound, and some of the most astute crouching I have ever seen was done by some of us trying to remain lost and hang on in the Pound when our parents came crowding around the wire fence to seek us out.

The Figure Eight was a magnet for most, with a high percentage of people who were driven half-mad by the uprush of wind caused by the sudden dips and turns of this contraption. One often saw respectable elders trying to stand up in the front seat of the roller coaster, plucking desperately at their layers of serge, their faces pale as death, slapping their hands to their brows, shouting 'Take me, O God,' and vowing never again to turn their back on Calvin.

The more daring hired bathing costumes. These articles had usually stretched with age and would have given a comfortable lift to a Zeppelin. The lads came thoughtfully out of the hiring shed, these shapeless blue robes hanging from them, looking like a gaggle of druids who have now decided to leave Wales the short way.

'Captain Webb, don't talk.'

'I like a bit of slack myself. I don't like those old tight things.'

'Watch my breast-stroke. What's the pier charge at Weston, boy?'

More than once these bathers laid themselves down on the water, faced in the general direction of the Somerset coast, gave a tremendous jerk of the legs and shot like torpedoes out of their costumes, to a salvo of cautionary shouts from clusters of deacons on the foreshore.

Patient fathers trailed behind their young through the teeming, fascinating booths of the fairground.

'Hey look, our Dad. Over there. Death of Crippen. What did he die of, Dad?'

'Lack of support, I suppose.'

Shorter days have never been. Through the first shadows we made the journey through the green vale back to the valley. In our compartment we lay thankful, silent, the air charged with the strange smells of repletion and sand. Even the desperate appeals of our mothers had grown weary, husky with acceptance.

'Merfyn, don't drop your rock in that gentleman's bowler.'

'Hold your chips out of the window, Bron. They're strong.'

'If it's more of that old pop you want, Prue, put your pinny on for pity's sake.'

And plain in the dusk was the face of fulfilment, gentle and wry.

*   *   *

59

Barry Island has been the jewelled eye in the childhood summers of millions of us, and from its docks has poured a quantity of coal large enough to have left at least three mountains in the north of the county quite hollow. There are few South Walians for whom Whitmore Bay and Bindles Ballroom have not furnished some hook of memory on which to hang a pleasant, evening thought.

Barry is, of course, a Jekyll and Hyde town. It developed rapidly into one of the finest Welsh ports, and it also had a stretch of sand that gave it the glamour of Bali for the herded troglodytes dreaming of the sea in the austere terraces of the valleys to the north. Now the docks have passed their zenith of wealth and power. The amount of coal passing through the dock gates would just about keep a vestry warm.

These facts have limelit the question of how much Barry should do to develop, consciously and expertly, its advantages as a resort. The debate is constant in the town and it evokes a good deal of eloquence and bad temper. The first essential fact seems to be that the holiday enterprises have always been very much a minority concern. The residential hotels of Barry are few and dispersed in such a way as makes it impossible for them to invoke that sense of fat jollity which you get from a string of luxury hotels. Any attempt to give Barry a spectacular new face would be hazardous and extraordinarily difficult. The cliffs to the west of Bindles Ballroom, with their rich meadows and luscious views of the Knap and the Island, have gone to private houses.

Other dreamers look hungrily at the great space made available by the filling in of the basin to the east of the Island causeway. Why not, they say, make the resort proper begin at Barry town, make the railway activities a little less obtrusive, and throw a handsome four-lane highway across to the Island, flanked by the best in hotels and theatres. The plan has sweep and force, but I suspect that by the time Barry will have found the finances the Bristol Channel will have moved away.

The present mode of entry to the Island is shockingly constricted. On a day of high festival the Island is as hard to get into as a bank at night. One side of the causeway has no pavement and I can count at least two neurasthenic citizens who grew so panicky at the endless whirring belt of cars and buses between The Ship Hotel and the Scenic Railway they threw themselves with relief into the Old Harbour.

On a sunny day show me a town that has not sent a coach to Barry and I will show you a town with a broken-down, Barry-bound coach being manhandled into making a start. There must be valley-towns where people keep coaches as they once kept rabbits. They come, too, from the

very centre of England. It is good to think of the Island doing its best to enrich the culture of the Midlands.

The Island for many Barrians, it would seem, is a kind of secret wound. From certain viewpoints, let me admit, the Island can be some-what rasping, but Barry has a dozen other places perfectly designed for the fastidious and the sensitive. The latter would rarely see the Island as anything but the Kingdom of the Chip, a hellish waste of candy floss, a romp of zanies wearing paper hats printed across with slogans of the most brazen tone. 'Come on, kid, I'm game.' The promenade tradesmen are regularly denounced as a covey of crafty horse-dealers who concede

The chip shop

to the town no fair proportion of their gains. The tradesmen angrily retort with a survey of their toil and risks. But the Island is part of the essential Barry. It is what it is because it is the biggest and nearest centre of colourful recreation for a huge industrial hinterland.

On first sight it looks as if you have stumbled on some section of humanity that has abandoned all activity but chewing. In these few acres at least the Welsh jaw has got its own back on the slump. The pattern has not changed greatly since the days of my Sunday school pilgrimages. The old Figure Eight in its new reddish casing looms above the fairground like a temple, and within its tunnelled dips and glides there is a constant litany of delighted gasps.

The mood now is altogether steadier, less apocalyptic, nourished into a nice numb jocosity by an abundance of shillings. There are the same inscrutable platoons of big-shouldered boys knocking the punch-balls so hard that slates drop off in Maesteg. The cafés bulge and the reign of the home-made sandwich is over. No more: 'I've brought the eight kids down with me but Redvers is coming on the next train with the food.' And Redvers would come into sight stooped like a yak under a package of sandwiches, vast and ill-tied, which would wait for Redvers to touch sand and then spill, ushering in a new era of rough chewing for the Celt.

I walked around the station to see the multitudes being entrained for home. The railway officials were as bland and obliging as ever they were with us. Not as many Sunday schools come now. You no longer get those days when the entire body of true believers in the Lower Rhondda descended like hail on the beaches of Barry. And the hour of return was like distribution-day in Heaven. 'Porth Congregationalists, Platform Three, ten past eight. Hafod Baptists, Platform Four, quarter to nine. Ynyshir Seventh Days, Platform One, any time now.' Once a group of wise alecks with me among them tried a simple jape. We approached the official and introduced ourselves: 'Blaencwm Buddhists.' Back shot the answer. 'Rickshaw from Penarth, two in the morning.'

I walked, at dusk, along the beach. I passed the very spot where in 1923 I almost drowned when serving as a short recruit in a human chain organised to stand in the sea and dredge with our toes for the teeth of the Sunday school Superintendent who had swum right out of his loose, hired costume, and had shot his dentures in an explosion of shame.

Whitmore Bay has a warm loveliness. Trample such a place as you may, beauty continues to have the tough persistence of the lugworm. As I stood there a cloud of children squealed in the last mad ecstasy of a long day's freedom. A circle of gulls waited patiently to re-inherit the silent beach and a few of them squawked about the day's litter. The fairground still hummed to staunch those very real hungers felt in lives that have been pressed squat by an excess of disciplined labour and social dreariness.

*   *   *

The country around Porthcawl is as fascinating a stretch of territory as you will find in the land. It is lapped in legend and lollies, warm with old romance and endless tea-urns. Joy with a widening wake of wafers.

Stand on the edge of Rest Bay and your eye can look on as vivid a contrast of scene and historic meaning as you can ever wish. To the left, way beyond the teeming sand-dwellers at Trecco Bay, is the curl of clifftop turf at Southerndown where once the wreckers of Dunraven plied their odd trade of swinging crafty lanterns to lure ships on to the rocks. They are gone, and the outfall at Ogmore is left to keep the balance of history right. To the west is that coastal strip of massive mills and darkening skies.

As a child I remember that one of the many moot points which kept the chapel elders in a constant state of feud was whether the annual treat should go to Barry Island or Porthcawl. Barry usually won. It was nearer. We felt more at home in the loose, lusty jacket of Whitmore Bay. Besides there was a suggestion of tone, dignity, even coldness about Porthcawl. The word 'Rest' always settled uneasily on creatures whose one aim in life was to deafen the world with the din of their delight.

And there was the matter of the wind. A gale seemed in those years to have got itself lost on Lock's Common. There was a tale told of a miner, enfeebled by illness and overwork to the lowest point of vitality. He went to the Miners' Rest at a time when the autumn gales were going into dress-rehearsal and they got the man well between their sights. Unless he had his stick driven six inches into the ground and a private tree to act as a windbreak, he could not stand erect. On his return to the Rest each day he had to be treated for excess air. But he was told: 'That's the beauty of the place, that's the value. It's so bracing.' The wind raced to a climax. He was picked up by a gust from Mumbles way one day and hurled against the rock face. He broke a collarbone but all he did was to get up and say, 'By God, it's bracing, like they said!'

And it's a lot more than that. As a holiday centre it obviously has a greater unity than Barry. South Wales suffers from a frightening lack of civilised hotels. We have too many hostelries that are little more than stews, where the conduct of people too often reflects the state of the

63

floors and counters. But these places that make up Porthcawl's West End aim at style and get there. They satisfy what should be a first require-ment of a holiday resort: they give the visitor a standard of amenity which he can use as a yardstick in his own town when he gets back there.

The miners of the central valleys had flooded into Porthcawl when I was there. The whole town was running with money and happiness. It was good to sit in the cool lounge of a hotel, thinking a shade sadly of all the leaping bits of joy that have been successfully gaffed in Wales in my lifetime. I listened because the voices of Glamorgan are strong and honest. One of them told the story of a neighbour from Maesteg who was in a caravan out on Trecco Bay, returning after an evening in and around the fairground. He had tried all the amusements, the Figure Eight, the chutes, the jet planes and every known brand of bottled beer. He got lost in the maze of dunes and caravans at Trecco and he wandered for an hour beneath the moon plaintively calling the name of his wife, and asking what had happened to Maesteg to make it so sandy. He continued this trek far into the night knocking on dozens of doors and windows calling out like the forsaken merman, 'Megan, Megan.' He did not find his wife on that trip but found five other women called Megan and got a fortnight in gaol for hindering sleep and undermining confidence.

Then the mood of the talk at the next table changed. Something in the ring of one of the phrases had reminded them of other things, other places. They began talking of 1926 and the rigours of the years that followed. But their faces continued to smile and shine. The bitterness had gone. The extra warmth and merriment that I could see all around me in Porthcawl had been added to their flesh, too.

The fairground has a spaciousness and order that the one at Barry has not got. It seems to have emerged from a single plan, and that from the mind of a man of quite brilliant gifts in this field. The central arena is ideally designed for boxing and for my own favourite bit of popular pageantry, the jazz band competitions, the gazooka bands that blew into glorious, uproarious life in the 1920's.

As I came into Porthcawl on the Tythegston road I drove behind a lorry on which a family with most of the furniture for a caravan was moving into quarters at Trecco. It was a striking tableau, because even on the lorry they were practically in residence. They were arranged quite cosily on chairs around a table, waving joyfully at all the passing traffic. As they turned off towards the dunes they were enveloped in brown dust. It was rather like a scene from *Grapes of Wrath*.

But the Trecco Bay caravan camp is an astonishing community by any standard. A little gritty in spots and irresistibly gay. But there will probably be hard thinking and debating about its future in planning circles. One thing is certain; whatever the final delicate balance of power between Sir Leslie Joseph and the local authority, Trecco Bay has made a valuable point. From now on the provision of large and relatively cheap holiday facilities for our people along the South Wales coast must be given urgent consideration. I will add in a mutter that when it comes to catering for the more frivolous requirements of humanity private enterprise can usually be relied on to bring home the bacon rather faster than the austere philosophy of the master-planners.

I went again to the fairground. These places fascinate the multitudes because they meet a hungry need. A bit of excitement, a bit of absurdity, a bit of noise, these are the slices of flavouring garlic in the broth of our normal experience. I followed a group of earnest, thoughtful lads from Ynyshir into the Chamber of Horrors. They tut-tutted gravely as they watched the various bits of creepiness laid out for their pleasure. They and I were riveted by a tableau of that doomed and diligent fellow, Christie, administering a dose of gas to a woman seated in a chair. One of the lads pointed at Christie. 'He's bald and he's got glasses,' he said as if these facts threw some light on the sable and terrifying antics going on waxily in front of us.

And his mate replied, 'I'm glad I stuck to darts.'

At mid-evening I walked back towards the town centre across that lovely stretch of turf flanked by grey rocks. Crowds were pouring towards the excellent pavilion for the evening concert. The sight of it brought to my mind the early autumn event which is bringing Porthcawl into the very centre of our best, living South Wales tradition, the miners' annual eisteddfod. This fetches all the gaiety and beauty down from the valleys. It has, for me anyway, a sweeter flavour than the more sombrely nationalist Eisteddfod that shuttles yearly between north and south.

Here, in early October, when the lights of Coney Beach are winking to their season's close, miners and their children reach a vocal splendour that causes even the dolphins in the bay to stand close in to shore and slap their fins. The time, the place, the people are all just right.

*   *   *

In miles, the run of railway between Carmarthen and Aberystwyth is not long. But its beauty is deep and varied, and you would not get a better chance of appreciating it if you were being pushed through it in a bath chair. This is, without question, the gentlest train in existence, the only railway on earth designed not to disturb the pollen in the lush paradise around. There is no bitterness in the faces of the cows that stare at you. They know it's going to take you two and a half hours to reach Aberystwyth and that's just about their tempo. I didn't actually see the engine take a chew at the grass, but it would have been in character.

There is nothing of the rip-roaring gaiety at Aberystwyth that you get at Barry and Porthcawl. Even about the amusements there is a hooded, rather furtive look. 'Knock three times and ask for Charles Gee.' The dodg'ems are indoors and under cover. In the slot-machine section on the pier youths stand with a look of suspicious distrust as if the last commandment they had received on leaving home had been not to unleash a penny without consulting a deacon. Or it may have been that right across the road from the entrance to the pier is a theological college.

Aberystwyth seems to be a town mainly of old people. The front is a stretch of prim but gracious late Victorian hotels, hinting to roisterers to muffle their joy or get shot in the bay. On their steps a large number of people sit in the sun, knitting, stroking cats and not saying much. They may, indeed must, get rapturous climaxes of gossiping, but whenever I passed they were in this tranquil slough.

On the front's north side is Constitution Hill which crumbles from time to time and causes problems. The cliff railway takes you to the top of the headland. The entrance to the railway is red brick and lowering, as if Dante might have been a founder-member. The earth around is like the brittler type of biscuit. The view from the top is magnificent, shadowed only by outcrops of that flaking shale and the memory of the house at the hill's bottom surrounded by the rubble of subsidence.

There has been talk of driving a tunnel through the headland to link up with the bays to the north. Of this there can be little hope. It would take the most tactful type of mole to drive a negotiable hole through that material. From a distance the headland looks disturbingly like one of the older South Wales tips. I add it to my list of whimsical Welsh hills that have taken a fancy to falling apart.

The beach lacks a rich sweep of sand. It is grey shingle crushed fairly fine by generations of holiday sitters. The sea moves very little this way or that, as if cured of all tidal frolics by the markedly earnest tone of the town. I would say that sitting on that shingle for several hours would make one thoughtful almost to the point of taking up Yoga.

A vigorous orchestra plays in the small concert pavilion. A big crowd sat listening in a safe, non-paying zone. It brought back to me an axiom

I heard from an ancient trouper: Mention Wales to anybody in show business and somebody wipes away a tear.

For the ear the place has every fascination. A large element of the holiday population comes over from the Midlands. They talk loudly because they are convinced that we cannot understand. Whenever I listened to them the topic was invariably the iron contrivance at the entrance to the women's wash-room into which the waiting ladies are fed like potatoes for chipping.

And the Welsh tongue itself is everywhere. In the lounge of my hotel two ageing Army officer types who looked as if they had only chosen Aberystwyth when Poona fell, were discussing the question of the native language. They would have talked about Urdu in the same bemused way. They would utter a phrase, then let the silence give it its final shape in the mind. One of them wanted to know why the old tongue had not died out. The other's eyes lit up.

'Damned garrulous lot, you know, these Welsh. Just haven't given the lingo a chance to lie decently down and die.'

I got up and raised in their direction my glass of watery grapefruit. I said, 'Gentlemen, I give you the restless, wagging tongue of Cymru, infinite in its guile to survive the calamities of shame and time.' My companion threw this into a passionate burst of Welsh.

The first Englishman looked at the other and said, almost compassionately, 'See what I mean?'

I ate in a café in the town's centre. The waitresses put a sisterly anxiety into their services. They recited the items on the menu in voices that made the humdrum inventory sound like '*Aderyn Pur*'. And they announced the price, clearly and with apology, before taking the order. I found this refreshing after several days in Central London ringed with ruthless restaurateurs all dreaming of winding up the season hung with rich, provincial pelts. That's mine, the third from the left, a little crumpled where I tried to hang on to a part of it. Not so in Aber.

I can still see the stolid face of one Midlander startled when the waitress bent right over him and told him with great reassurance, 'And don't worry about the cakes. They are in with the chips.'

The University College at the southern end of the front is one of our proudest creations. From the outside it is rather sombre, somewhat like an Oxford college caught in misalliance with a chapel. A group of young Army cadets from the North examined the college with interest as if it were some latent holiday gimmick from whose top an organist would shortly emerge. They sought information about the inlaid illustrations that stand high up on the college's southern wall.

I explained to them that the pictures symbolised the will of the common folk to a richer culture, a fuller mastery over life. This, on top of the heat, was too much for the cadets. They took off their caps to let the cool air on to their heads. Then they ambled off to the pier.

The high golden moment for me was my trip up the Rheidol Valley. I travelled in the classic style, and let no one fob you off with car or bus or yak. I went by the miniature railway, the 'Mabinogion Flyer'. For the last thirty minutes of this prodigious climb Nature throws at you everything she has in the line of chastening splendour. I travelled in an open carriage, too near the engine. The smell and the noise were excessive. I think a little electrification and a polite brush-off to Stephenson and Watt would be in order here.

Just in front of me sat a father, mother and son. The boy was sitting with his limbs unnaturally still and his face as impassive as the seat. The father said, 'Look at Mansel. He's going pale green with the height and the cold.' The mother gave the boy a mild shake. 'What's the matter, Mansel? You bad?' Mansel struggled up from deep torpor. His body shook in rhythm with the train's every vibration. 'I'm numb with the chugging,' he said.

At Devil's Bridge I looked around at that massive nest of green serenity. Too much awe can be bad medicine and I found a smiling relief, some hours later, in strolling up and down the Aberystwyth promenade in the first hour of darkness.

I listened to the laughter of bathers diving from rafts in the shadowed bay. Beneath the coloured lights crowds played out all the games that love and boredom have ever suggested to the wit of man.

5 Self-Improvement

HOW TO BECOME A WELSH COMMITTEE MAN

On Belmont Square.

VIRGIL VAUGHAN (*an intense, whip-voiced megalomaniac*): Now look, Denzil, you were right to come to me. In committee work lies the future of man. Lash enough committees together and you have a raft that will take you to any pinnacle. Never mind what the committee is, join it. If it isn't there, start it.

DENZIL HUGHES: Yes.

VIRGIL: Watch me. The only committee in Belmont that I'm not on is the W.V.S. and the various sisterhoods, but even there I'm on hand as an adviser on procedure. You'll make enemies.

DENZIL: Ay.

VIRGIL: There was that Alderman Phipps last night. 'Virgil Vaughan,' he told me, 'you've got agenda poisoning. Look at you twice and you read the agenda of the last meeting.' That's what Alderman Phipps said.

DENZIL: He's bitter beyond, Phipps.

VIRGIL: You've got the right face, Denzil. Round and a bit innocent. My face is a bit sharp and my voice is on the masterful side, so they tell me. But once they look at you they'll vote you into positions of confidence at once.

DENZIL: I'm looking forward to that, Virgil.

VIRGIL: They'll think you're a bit of a poor dab and they'll think you'll be an easy mark to handle. Let them think that until you've got your hand firmly on the rudder of the committee.

DENZIL: On the what?

VIRGIL: Never mind. Now then, how much knowledge of committee work have you got?

DENZIL: Not much, Virgil. You know me. Very quiet sort of life. Darts, the pigeons, making mats with that little wool machine, and the male voice party. And I had to go sparing with the party when the wool from the mats made me sneeze in the middle of the longer notes.

VIRGIL: Weren't you on any sort of committee, ever? (*There is a note of marvelling in Virgil's voice. Denzil is clearly to him a freak.*)

DENZIL: Don't think so.

VIRGIL: You'll be superb material. Clay that has never been fingered, under my touch. You'll be the finest shunter of amendments in this zone.

DENZIL: (*diffidently*): Oh . . .

VIRGIL: What is it now?

DENZIL: I remember, I was on a sort of committee once.

VIRGIL: Did you intervene actively? Were you dynamic? Did you have any of your motions carried?

DENZIL: Oh, no. It was a Christmas Club in that little pub, The Crossed Harps. One night just before the feast the treasurer asked me to slip down to the station and ask the times of the trains to London. I did. Wrote them down. He left the next day with the funds. Never saw him again.

VIRGIL: That was a negative experience. Don't bother to recall it. And if ever a treasurer or any official asks you to go down the station again, ignore him. Stick at the table.

DENZIL: I'll be there like glue, Virgil. Any mention of the station and I'll know they're up to something.

VIRGIL: Now then as a committee man, there are certain words you've got to learn to use. Some of these words have taken on a kind of magic power. You can throw them like bullets or poleaxes. The average committee man never feels absolutely secure about the laws of the game he is playing. In the middle of a long discussion, with a headfull of rhetoric and a bellyfull of cliches, he wonders whether it was worth humanity's while coming out of the cave just for that. And if you see a committee man holding out against you, just ask him for an elucidation of the procedural gambits of the last half hour. He'll go flatter than the lino.

DENZIL: Gambits. I'll remember that. And elucidation. I'll be in there every whipstitch demanding that.

VIRGIL: Keep the dust flying. If you feel they've got you in a corner, shout suddenly at some member who is a bit of a book reader: 'The bristles of your dialectic are crossed and stiff, friend. Dip them in the turps.'

DENZIL: Bristles. Turps. I won't forget that. I've done a bit of decorating. First class for clogged bristles, turps. Teach me some of these words that send people scattering like chaff, Virgil.

VIRGIL: I'm full of them. Here's a good one. 'Tighten up that syllogism, friend, your false premises are showing.' I attended that philosophy class at the Educational Settlement for five years. I used to look after the register and make the tea. And some of these ikey so-and-so's used to say, 'That Virgil Vaughan is a witless creep. All he's fit for is to keep the register and bring us biscuits when we're half-dead with logic and blinded by mental light. He doesn't follow the lecture for a minute. He'd have to be in the water to tell Plato from plankton.' That's what they said. But they were wrong, Denzil. Virgil Vaughan was behind them like a *milgi*, like a police dog. I learned words in that class that have set icicles of uneasiness hanging over a thousand committee tables.

DENZIL: Teach me the words, Virgil. Couple of voters about here I'd like to put on edge, I can tell you.

VIRGIL: Never be too simple. As a committee man you'll have to listen to more clotted nonsense than the human ear was built to stand. You've got to dilute it a bit. And if you are listening to someone who sounds to you as if he took his brain off with his bowler you'll be tempted to say, 'That's daft.' Don't say it. It's too rough, too fundamental. You've got to keep up the illusion of committee work as a game of skill.

DENZIL: What do I do, Virgil? Just sit there and shut up?

VIRGIL: Never do that, Denzil. Never shut up. Even if you sit there mumbling bits from 'The Shooting of Dan MacGrew', do that, to convince them that you're still in the field, shooting hard for goal. But never be too harsh when rebuking daftness. Or too subtle. Once when I was just starting I tried to persuade the Parks Committee that they needed something a bit brisker than bowls and a bit plusher than metal seats if the parks were to broaden the smile of the town. And also a brand of park-keeper less dour and vigilant, less apt to creep up behind hedges and prod lovers out of their rapture and send them home at the double.

DENZIL: Bad thing, that. Had some. Shock for the system. Shouldn't be allowed. Glad you spoke up against it, Virgil. Trust you.

VIRGIL: I demanded enclosed arbours, specially warmed. Also gondolas for the lake with cushions and a special grant for the town band to get sheet music with a Venetian flavour.

Rugby game

DENZIL: Just right that. Change from the overture to 'Zampa' they're always playing. And those gondolas are a bit posh too. Seen them in pictures down at the Alcazar. Canoodling fit to kill on the cushions and a tenor in the prow rowing and singing.

VIRGIL: The chairman of the committee was that very craggy and negative moralist, my uncle, Alderman Hesketh Vaughan the Veto.

DENZIL: I know him. Brows like fur and eyes like monumental marbles. Put paid to more passion than the common cold in his time.

VIRGIL: He started calling me Lot, and asked if I was now standing for Sodom or Gomorrah.

DENZIL: And him with his knowledge of the wards.

VIRGIL: So I decided to give him back as good as he had given. A Biblical joke in committee can often silence or paralyse you. Either answer with another Biblical joke or, if nothing occurs to you in that line, fall back on wit. That's what I did. Fell back on wit.

DENZIL: What wit was this now, Virgil?

VIRGIL: I said they were the first group of elected blockheads ever officially to exchange acne for woodworm.

DENZIL (blankly): Oh!

VIRGIL: My uncle Hesketh said that under standing orders he had the right to have every joke explained.

DENZIL: Fair enough. Pretty deep, that about the woodworm.

VIRGIL: By the time I had finished explaining we had forgotten what the original motion was. Even *I* supported a proposal that wit be abolished.

DENZIL: Agree there. Too flashy, that wit, too sharp. If it's a cleaner world we want, Virgil, give me a brush before a knife. I'll remember all this. Don't be harsh, don't be brilliant. And what is the tactic with fools, Virgil?

VIRGIL: There are several fine phrases that will make a man feel that he's been talking through the top of his slouch. For example you might say: 'This is Gilbertian.' Always stand up when you say that and give a great cracking laugh to remind the slower members that you are referring to Gilbert the well-known comic writer.

DENZIL: Oh *that* Gilbert. Gilbertian. That's good.

VIRGIL: Or you might say: 'This is a travesty of the facts.' But don't laugh when you say that. Or 'This is a squalid contravention of the truth,' and stay straight-faced for that one too.

DENZIL: Right. Travesty. Squalid contravention. And stay solemn.

VIRGIL: And this is a good one, too. 'This is the logic of Alice.'

DENZIL: Charlie Alliss, the Independent?

VIRGIL: No, no. Alice, the girl in the looking glass, the wonderland girl.

DENZIL: Oh aye. I'll remember these terms, Virgil. I'll try them out on Edith tonight.

The kitchen of Denzil Hughes.

DENZIL: Now, fair's fair, Ede. I'll grant you it's hot and it's tasty. But it's monotonous. Too much of a good thing.

EDITH HUGHES: What is now?

DENZIL: This craze for cheese. Last night, cheese and egg. Breakfast this morning, cheese and bacon. Dinner time today, cheese and chop. Now tonight, cheese and chips. Have we got cows at last?

EDITH: So you're tired of cheese, are you? The future mayor is flagging over his favourite dish.

DENZIL: I'm only saying it's coming a bit frequent. It's not a food any more. I'm wearing it like a suit. Too rich.

EDITH: And whose fault is that, Denzil Hughes? Who kept nodding and saying 'Hear, Hear' when that clown, Virgil Vaughan, sat in that very chair and said no man could hope to become a rounded orator without one good cheese dish a day?

DENZIL: Virgil knows. He's rounded.

EDITH: And that set you to darting into the grocer's every time you passed the shop to get a half pound. The pantry's full of it. We've got two queues of mice, and the cat is giddy with the smell.

DENZIL: All right. I over-bought. I was too zealous. I've got ambition. There's too much cheese in the larder. But cheese for every meal, it's . . . it's Gilbertian! (*Gives the loud cracking laugh prescribed by Virgil for use with this adjective.*)

EDITH: It's what?

DENZIL: It's Gilbertian. (*He repeats the laugh.*)

EDITH: Are you delirious, Denzil? What are you laughing at?

DENZIL: It's a travesty of the facts and it's a squalid . . . something . . . of the truth.

EDITH: What are you talking about?

DENZIL (*speaking indistinctly through a mouthful of food*): It's the logic of Alice.

EDITH: Just lower the cheese barrier a bit. I can't hear you. And that makes a nice change, I can tell you. The dart-board must have fallen on your head down at the Crossed Harps. Just wait there while I get somebody to wheel you off. You're raving. That last bit of cheese finished you off.

DENZIL: These are just phrases that Virgil Vaughan has taught me. I'm sitting on my first committee next Tuesday and I'm getting used to the feel of them between my teeth.

EDITH: Stick to chips and grunting, Denzil. You'll be safer.

A committee, convened for no very brilliant reason, is assembling in a room in the Bannerman Club.

VIRGIL (*more tense and conspiratorial than ever*): There's the chairman, my uncle, Alderman Hesketh Vaughan the Veto. He'll want the meeting over in a jiffy so that he can manage a game of crib and a last jug in the club. That's how corrupt ageing committee men can become.

DENZIL: Never thought to find such weakness of the flesh in Hesketh Vaughan the Veto.

VIRGIL: Look at the angle of his eyebrows. It means an amendment will have to be faster than Guto Nyth Bran to slip under his defences.

DENZIL: He's frowning like anything at me. What's that for?

VIRGIL: Think nothing of it. He's got eyebrows. So he's using them. He believes in keeping everybody on edge. It's a tactic with Uncle Hesketh.

ALD. HESKETH VAUGHAN (*in a malignant mutter*): How did that Virgil Vaughan get on this committee? He spreads like dry rot.

CHARLIE ALLISS: When the notion of this committee was first mooted to discuss the problem of delinquent youth, Virgil gave an address down at the Old Aged Pensioners Club. I was there. He was on top form. He had them nursing their mastoid bone, I can tell you. He was on about the central problem facing both the young and the old, loneliness it was. They suggested the formation of this committee and voted Virgil on to it just to shut him up. He took some of the aged down to a rock-and-roll session at the Youth Club. Bullied a few of them into joining in. Almost broke their backs.

HESKETH: Take back what I said about dry rot. At least that's quiet. I don't like that chap with him either. That Denzil Hughes. It wasn't so bad as long as we could feel that Virgil was on his own. A rare germ. Deadly, but on his own. Now he's got an echo, this Hughes. How did *he* get on to any committee. Dull as a bat, I always thought. Got a very poor record. He failed as a pigeon fancier because he couldn't give the pigeons the sort of bright look they want to come home to.

CHARLIE: It was last week at the preliminary meeting. The room was a bit smoky and there was a racket coming from the snooker room next door. We were all a bit foxed, being half-choked and with the noise and all that. Virgil got up to say something. We thought he said, 'I move we get someone to clean the flues,' and we passed it unanimously. What he said was, 'I move that we co-opt Denzil Hughes.'

HESKETH: The world would be safer without rhymes of any description. You certainly pushed the wrong brush up there, all right.

HESKETH: Well, gentlemen, we'll make a start. And with a little co-operation from all sides we should proceed swiftly through the night's business. (*His tone is very sweet, even deliberately anaesthetic.*)

VIRGIL (*in fairly noisy whisper to Denzil*): See the tactic? The honeyed tone, the drip of ether, lulling us into complacency.

HESKETH: Mr Vaughan, please. If you'd like the gavel and the chair, say so.

VIRGIL: I was just making an *ad hoc* observation to my friend, Mr Denzil Hughes.

DENZIL: That's right. Just a bit of *ad hoc* from one friend to another.

HESKETH: Now then, gentlemen. Let's explain the reason for the convening of this committee. There's been a lot of fuss lately about the behaviour of the young, the rise in offences by juveniles and so on. There's been a hue and cry in the local press and speaking legally I don't think a prima facie case has been made out against the youth. I think a lot of wild statements have been made.

VOICE: I object.

VIRGIL and DENZIL (*Denzil's voice very hesitant and low*): Hear, hear.

HESKETH: What is it, Mr Crawley?

NICHOLAS CRAWLEY (*voice is a hammock swinging between righteousness and neurasthenia*): The chairman knows that I started that correspondence. The chairman is an ostrich.

VIRGIL and DENZIL: Hear, hear.

CRAWLEY: And he must have got his head stuck in some special quality sand to see so little of what's going on around him, so little of the bruise that is darkening the decency of our social life.

VIRGIL and DENZIL: Hear, hear.

VIRGIL (*urgently*): Pitch it up a bit there, Denzil.

VIRGIL and DENZIL (*much more robustly*): Hear, hear.

HESKETH: Why don't you two switch to the Anvil Chorus?

VIRGIL: You've got a very piercing point there, Mr Crawley. Don't be talked down.

CRAWLEY: The streets of this town are infested at night by bands of brazen pagans.

1ST VOICE: Marauding rodneys.

2ND VOICE: Chewing apes.

1ST VOICE: Jackets down to their knee-caps. Crepe soles up to their ankles.

2ND VOICE: Sideboards down to their shoulders.

CRAWLEY: Wilful jostling and obscene shouting on every hand. A band of them broke into a session of the Old English, Old Style Dancing Group at the Eldorado Hall. Locked the M.C. up in a small closet and turned the place into a Babylon of stamping and yelling. The M.C. is still weak, still on a diet of nerve tonic and the quieter waltzes.

1ST VOICE: Girls and women afraid to walk alone in the darker streets. I demand flood-lights or platoons of vigilantes. Woman in Bessemer Crescent, coming home from chip shop with chips for supper, chased by one of these young louts; he was in drink, his eyes like headlamps, his hair all waves, chased that woman for fifteen minutes, she reached home panting and alarmed, chips stone cold.

2ND VOICE: Threw two bandsmen bodily into the lake when the band on their request night decided to play 'Rock of Ages' instead of 'Rock, Rock, Rock'.

VOICES: Shameful. Wicked. That shows. That's proof.

1ST VOICE: When they buy shoes they buy one pair for walking and another for kicking.

CRAWLEY: We want the stocks back.

HESKETH: The what?

CRAWLEY: The stocks, the pillory. Legs through holes and exposed to shame.

1ST VOICE: You're right. The stocks. A fillip to the local carpentry trade which is currently in the doldrums, and the chance of a return to the kind of virtue we learned at our mothers' knees.

VOICES: Lock them up. Nail them down. Bring back the birch.

CHARLIE: Now wait a minute.

HESKETH: Mr Charlie Alliss has the floor.

CHARLIE: Let's calm down a bit. We all had high spirits when we were young. Give the youngsters a bit of fair play. All the atrocities you've mentioned here tonight were quite common when we were kids.

CRAWLEY: I challenge Mr Charlie Alliss on that point. Things were NOT the same when we were young. The only bandsman I ever saw in full uniform in the rowing lake had thrown himself in, had gone in of his own accord after playing three wrong notes in the 'Dead March from Saul' while escorting the late mayor to the Black Meadow. And the only woman in my memory to be chased while carrying chips was chased by a man who was genuinely hungry for chips.

CHARLIE: Call Crawley to order, Mr Chairman. His hinges are melting.

HESKETH: Now then, gentlemen, do you mind if I sprinkle a little coolness? I'm grateful to the people who called for this committee but I think some of them are suffering from what I might call committeeman's twitch.

1ST VOICE: What's that, Alderman?

CRAWLEY: You don't see me twitching. Face and hands steady as a rock.

HESKETH: It's a complaint that makes a committee man certain that nothing in the world is being done about the problem he is discussing outside the room where he sits. I think Mr Crawley sees humanity in too lurid a light. You'll always have a few clowns who'll chase their neighbours. But they grow tired and respectable and eventually they learn to sit down like the rest of us. I vote we leave the whole matter on the table, adjourn this committee *sine die* and send a short note of confidence to the police, the churches and the youth clubs who are already doing quite well what this committee is setting itself up to do.

VIRGIL (*his voice ringing with wrathful irony*): Mr Chairman!

CRAWLEY: Speak for Belmont, Virgil.

1ST VOICE: Speak up for the virtues we learned at our mother's knee or didn't the alderman's mother have a knee?

2ND VOICE: Bring back the birch. A thong for every thug. An eye for an eye and a noose for a sideboard.

VIRGIL: The alderman has become a sexton. Leave it on the table, he says. Adjourn *sine die*, he says. If the universe were reduced to ash the alderman would be there with his little brush to sweep it under the carpet out of sight.

DENZIL: It's Gilbertian.

VIRGIL: He is a thrombotic clot in the vein of our civic awareness and he will be chuckling when the conscience of Belmont suffers its final stroke.

DENZIL: It's the logic of Alice. Not you, Charlie.

VIRGIL: The situation, as my friend, Mr Denzil Hughes, has just said, is Gilbertian. On the one hand the alderman sucks his opium and says nothing. On the other hand you have the prophets of wrath, the avenging-bolt collectors, the wild-eyed, the Puritans, who have sex crimes as consistently before their eyes as other people have spots or glasses. The alderman wants public life to be a licensed coma. The others want the cat o'nine tails, the rack and so much penal rope we'd have to switch the national economy from coal to hemp.

79

HESKETH: You've got the floor, Mr Vaughan. And if I know you you'll
  have two of the walls as well before you finish. All right, guide us.

VIRGIL: You want to be dynamic. You can't ignore these young
  hooligans. Nor can you whip them back into the vestry virtues of
  yester-year.

1ST VOICE: Spare the whip, sink the ship.

2ND VOICE: Spare the rope, give up hope.

VIRGIL: Do you wear matching collars with your hair shirts? Get a
  little joy, brothers, get a little joy.

DENZIL: That's it. Unbend, boys, unbend. You're rigid beyond.

VIRGIL: Be creative. Be positive. That principle has always guided my work as a committee man. Let me put this whole matter into a nut-shell. These youths have no sense of community service.

HESKETH: What's that you say?

VIRGIL: Community service. The sense of living through love of one's neighbours.

HESKETH: This is pure oratorio. This man is a pixie. He's taken all the happiness out of committee work for me. Not content with sending a thousand tidy agendas reeling to the canvas he is now in the market for miracles. Let me tell you something, Virgil, my boy. If you can inspire any neighbourly love in that pack of wolfish rodneys it will be the most remarkable operation since the man who claimed to bring youth back with the glands of monkeys. How do you propose to do it? Hypnotism or a grafting of membrane from the saintlier missionaries?

VIRGIL: Simple. I will go to these boys. I will approach them as one of themselves. I will wear a bright check shirt to show that I understand their innocent wish to be bright and distinctive. I will even listen to the gramophone records they favour even if it means having a crack open right across my tympanum. I will let my hair grow at the back and I will get my sister, Letitia, who has a home perm set, to arrange a few waves. But I will point out to the boys that I am doing this more in imitation of Lloyd George than in tribute to them. You see how you slip a sly bit of education into the most unlikely occasion.

HESKETH: That will be worth watching. Charlie Alliss here is an out-fitter. He'll let you have the shirt free. And make it a tight one, Charlie. Virgil breathes too easily.

CHARLIE: I've got a real screamer in the window. Yellow, red and blue. Just the job, Virgil. It's made to be worn outside the trousers.

VIRGIL: Anything for social progress, even an unaccustomed coolness about the waist. I will even chew gum.

HESKETH: That'll be a change from the fat I've heard you chewing on the fifteen committees you've taken over in this town.

VIRGIL: Then I shall introduce a sadder note into my talk with these boys. I will tell them that while I respect their wish for gaiety and flippancy there is more to life than that. I will take them on a tour of the side-streets. I will show them the lonely, the aged, the deprived of this town. They will touch the colder edges of life. They will begin to ask me how they can help these poor exiles whose fire-places are a drift of old, cold ash.

HESKETH: By this time they will have given up chewing gum. They will be nibbling directly at you.

81

VIRGIL: I want a community service centre set up, stocked with wood and tools and instructors. The lonely and deprived will have told the youths of little articles that would make for their greater comfort. And the youths will make them. Before you know it they'll be as sober and responsible as the old-style deacons. I propose that a sub-committee be set up to solicit support for the new community service centre.

DENZIL: I second that motion, Mr Chairman. I feel it a privilege to second that motion so ably proposed by Mr Virgil Vaughan.

HESKETH: All right, Denzil. Don't make a carol of it. You've seconded the motion. Show of hands, please. For. Against. The ayes have it. You've got your sub-committee, Virgil.

1ST VOICE: I propose the alderman as chairman of the sub-committee.

VIRGIL: Without any disrespect to the alderman I think that on this sub-committee we should have only activists, dedicated men.

2ND VOICE: I second the alderman. A prince of chairmen, the alderman. Any committee set up in Belmont without him would be hopping about on a crutch.

HESKETH: Vote. . . . Right. Thank you. I'll want to be there to see how it works out, Virgil. When you let loose those hooligans on the old and the lonely with acts of charity and carpentry I will personally recommend the old and the lonely to duck or move on to the next town.

In foreground a man running for his life with angry men in pursuit.

DENZIL: In here, Virgil, in here.

VIRGIL (*in explosive distress*): Thank you, Denzil. Now you see that the path of public service is not always smooth.

DENZIL: You're panting hard there, Virgil. What happened?

VIRGIL: You know that I've been trying to win the confidence of the corner boys.

DENZIL: You look the part, Virgil. A daring stroke. That's a fine shirt that Charlie Alliss gave you. The colours are a bit harsh or that may be because you're so pale after the running. And those waves in your hair at the back. They're a treat although they seem to be running in the wrong direction. They are a credit to your sister's home-perming set. Makes the top half of your head look like Weston Pier.

VIRGIL: Thank you, Denzil. I've gone all out to convince those lads that I can share their outlook. I got a guitar. Made my finger-tips bleed. All we Vaughans have tender digits but it showed them I was willing. Got these drain-pipe trousers, too. Belonged to my grandfather.

Thirty-five years old. Made such a hit at the time there were three funerals bidding for him at once. Best serge. Too tight though. Makes me feel trapped.

DENZIL: Like teak. Never wear out. A fine judge of serge, your grand-father.

VIRGIL: Even got one of those flick knives to use in a talk I was going to give the boys against the use of these pernicious weapons. Went off in my trousers pocket while I was fiddling for change. Flick, just like that. A shock, I can tell you. A man doesn't know what to do for the best.

DENZIL: Bad, that. Especially when you're fiddling for change. Makes you cold to think about it.

VIRGIL: I was with them tonight. I had been giving them some pre-liminary talk on the old and outcast people of the earth, beginning with the Eskimos and finishing with those two very old pensioners up in Inkerman Row who haven't been out of the house for eight years.

DENZIL: Home birds, those two. Been touchy about going out ever since they had fireworks stuck into the bands of their slouches after a lecture at the Institute.

VIRGIL: One of the lads denounced me as a sentimental square, a moral Victor Silvester. They dared me to join them in whistling amorously at two passing girls.

DENZIL: That showed their impudence. Asking a committee man of your calibre to show his passion in the main street.

VIRGIL: It was a hard test. I'll say that. I hate whistling and as for passion I've got that taped and tidy. I'm engaged to an honourable and upright girl, Miss Prudence Pugh, granddaughter of Franklin Pugh, the old colliery manager and a close associate of Nicholas Crawley in the fight against hooliganism.

DENZIL: Know them well. Big house. Granite pillars in the porch. A mansion. But a crotchety voter, Pugh.

VIRGIL: I overdid the whistle. I didn't realise I had so much wind in me. It was a sound of shattering power. It sent the girls scattering like sparrows and it brought Nicholas Crawley and his posse of vigilantes, who were patrolling two streets away, rushing up at the double. I took off. The louts stayed where they were and assured the vigilantes that I was the ringleader, their tutor in lust and whistling, the hub of many a squalid affray. The Crawley platoon got nearer. I could hear Crawley muttering the very number of the hymn that would be sung curtly at my funeral.

DENZIL: An unmatched grasp of the hymnal, Crawley, fair play.

VIRGIL: I dived into the house of my fiancée, Miss Prudence Pugh. She was not there. But her grandfather was there. The light was poor. And the old man's short-sighted and a bit deaf. He wouldn't have been able to hear my explanations when I came rushing into his passage, even if I had had the breath to make them. He thought I must be an assassin sent by the corner boys to deal with him after his last letter to the *Bulletin*. It was signed 'Outraged' but you can tell a Franklin Pugh letter by the smoke that comes out of the commas.

DENZIL: Read it. A scorcher. Must use a relief nib fixed into a gas poker. But I bet Franklin Pugh recognised you in a flash, made you welcome and showed you his next letter.

VIRGIL: Would I have come shooting into your kitchen like a persecuted setter if he had? He might have recognised me though. I showed him up once in a committee where he showed no grasp of procedure and he might have been waiting for just that chance. He tripped me up in the passage and let me have one across the back of the head with the handle of a broom. An old-fashioned broom. They don't make them like that any more. Like a telegraph post. He's fussy about cleanliness in the home. Forever sweeping. That's why he had that broom handy. I lurched out of his place bandy-legged as a jockey, all my head-bones singing *Calon Lan*. But does this mean defeat?

DENZIL: In my case it would, Virgil. Being chased by Crawley's whippets, then clipped with a brush. I'd go back to darts.

VIRGIL: That's because you've never had the true taste of power, the kingly feeling that the chairmanship of a good committee can give you. Wait till you've had the gavel in your hand like a hammer of doom. Wait till you've scuttled the whole opposition with half a dozen amendments. The first meeting of the sub-committee is in a fortnight and we'll be ready for them.

Village Hall. On stage a very raffish rock and roll group is beating out the butt end of a loose musical arrangement.

CHAIRMAN: Thank you, Billy Bush and his Belmont Beaters, five local boys who show that Kentucky has nothing on the Celts.

1ST VOICE: The one with the washing-board is coming forward.

2ND VOICE: To say he's sorry, I bet. His beat was very poor. He could really have been washing clothes with it. Dropped it twice.

1ST VOICE: He's older than the others. Look, it's Virgil Vaughan.

VIRGIL: Ladies and gentlemen, you are probably surprised to see me appear before you in the costume of a generation slightly younger than my own.

VOICES: Yes.

VIRGIL: And you may be wondering about this wash-board in my hand.

1ST and 2ND VOICES: Yes.

VIRGIL: It is not intended as an instrument of music. It is the symbol of a world shortly to be purified by a new ideal of social service among the young, a symbol of the dreams of goodness among our youth that have as yet been given no proper outlet.

Billy Bush rocks into a new number.

1ST VOICE: That's right, Billy. Shut him up. He's bad for the beat.

2ND VOICE: He's quite right, though. An hour in or at the tub would do the world of good to some of these Teds.

A committee room.

CHARLIE ALLISS: Is he making progress?

HESKETH VAUGHAN: Progress! He's persuaded half a dozen bodies to set up social welfare sub-committees. He's been on T.V. Three close-ups of his grandfather's trousers, two of the waves at the back of his head, and one of the finger-tips he lacerated on that wretched washing-board. He's talked Bethel Chapel into letting him have the use of their old P.T. hut. And he is taking his squad of social regenerates around in a pack to bring company and good cheer to the aged and lonely. They are a new hazard on what was already a pretty rough

85

road. The aged and lonely are bound by courtesy to offer this flood of well-wishers a cup of tea and some cake. They are being eaten out of house and home. Vaughan is creating a new crisis of hunger and want among the poor and the aged.

Group of youths led by Vaughan leaving the tiny cottage of Mrs Prosser, an old aged pensioner.

VIRGIL: And I'll say this, Mrs Prosser. The tea was as strong as your own brave heart.

MRS PROSSER (*in a voice streaked with age but with an edge of caustic intelligence*): Six spoonfuls in the pot. As much as I'd use in a week without callers. But I see the point of what you had to say about the dangers of loneliness, Mr Vaughan . . . still, six spoonfuls . . .

VIRGIL: And those salmon sandwiches. Fresh as dew. And Welsh cakes fit for a Prince of Wales.

VARIOUS MIXED GRUFF VOICES OF THE YOUTHS: The sandwiches were tip-top. The salmon was a treat.

MRS PROSSER: It was a dearer brand than I get as a rule. They were all out of the cheap brand. Glad you liked it. Wish I'd got to the plate before you finished.

VIRGIL: I bet it's given you a new lease of life, Mrs Prosser, to have provided so amply for the boys. I can assure you that the sight of your hospitality will light up their lives for many days to come.

MRS PROSSER: Oh, they ate very well. They've got very good teeth, Mr Vaughan. Now if you'd care to leave a little something for the mice . . .

A committee room.

VIRGIL: Now, Mr Alderman, dare to say that a new flame of enthusiasm has not been lit among youths who a few weeks ago were dangerously feckless and anti-social.

HESKETH: I know. Flame is right. I've been seeing some of the charred victims. That voter with extreme stiffness of the limbs, Cadmon Crewes the Creak. Your apostles made Crewes a special type of chair, bed and lectern so that Crewes could read, rock or repose as the fancy took him. The chair is delivered. Crewes is lowered into it with a lack of confidence that would have gone down well in Sing Sing. Crewes, after about ten minutes' coaxing, pushes the lever that should bring the book-rest into position. Every part of the chair begins to move and clank. They took an hour to get Crewes free and he's been standing up ever since laughing and crying every whipstitch. Then there was that man, Willie Clapham. His coal-house went west in the last gale. Your boys threw up a rough structure to shelter Clapham's exposed load. Clapham has been trying to borrow coal ever since and badgering you for the combination that will let him in to get at his own fuel.

VIRGIL: Very unco-operative, Clapham. Doesn't know a nice, tight little waterproof structure when he sees one.

HESKETH: And those two young outlaws who tried to tunnel across the main street to get at the vaults of the bank. In between shifts they'd nip back to your social service centre for a strong cocoa and a new load of wooden props for the tunnel. Now let's leave all that nonsense. Let's get our heads down from the clouds and discuss a simple, straightforward bit of kindliness. How large a cheque should we send to the old-aged pensioners for their annual summer outing? Thirty pounds. Any objections? What is it now, Virgil?

VIRGIL: Just to show you, Alderman, that my head, though a little bruised, is unbowed. With the sort of cheap libels we have just been hearing, you destroyed what might have been the finest educational experiment since Thomas Charles of Bala. Bethel Chapel has padlocked its hut and Cadmon Crewes has told me that he gets a rash every time he sets eyes on wood.

HESKETH: And good luck to him, poor dab. Where once he saw a simple chair he now sees a potential gibbet.

VIRGIL (*with a deep, plangent sadness in his voice*): It's all so simple for you, Alderman. Thirty pounds for the old-aged, you say. For their summer treat. And that's off your conscience again. No thought of bringing them more firmly into the main stream of our social delight.

DENZIL: Tell us about this stream, Virgil. Tell us about delight.

A groan from Alderman Hesketh Vaughan.

CHARLIE (*in a mutter*): I told you that we should have sent that Denzil to the middle of Africa as part of a package deal with the Missionary League.

VIRGIL: I am thinking of the Annual Sports and Gala this year. I've got here the blue print of a small coracle which was drawn for me by a gifted boy at the social community centre before it was torpedoed by the malign and the unimaginative. The old folk would find this coracle easy and cheap to make. Now, if instead of the very stale items that have been overloading the programme of the gala for years past we could stage a coracle race for the over-sixties on the River Moody . . .

HESKETH: Have you got your gun with you, Charlie?

6 A Clutch of Perished Bards

W. H. DAVIES

To be Welsh is, in many ways, tough. To be a Welsh poet in a world so jaggedly Philistine, that is really hitting rock. I am assuming W. H. Davies to be Welsh but I do not think he would have agreed. He spoke no Welsh and as we see from *Poet's Pilgrimage*, a small volume of travel memories written in his post-tramp stage, he took an almost Norman view of the West Walians. He was slightly more charitable in his judgment of the people of Glamorgan and Monmouthshire, but that was only because they stood a whit nearer in speech and manner to the fat little villages of Wiltshire and Gloucestershire which he loved so much.

Poets get off to a rugged start. They are conscious of carrying within themselves a precious creative charge in which no more than a handful of people are going to be interested. There is no field of art in which so much pure intelligence is going to be expended for so little return. Indeed I can see the day when inbred potencies are listed and charted at birth. Those in danger of a tumble with the muse will be given an instant shot of whatever hormones make a man a satisfied fair-ground barker. At least your message there is going to be more generally understood.

The poet is born with a gift of such heightened sensibility that half the time he needs a police dog to find the top of his head; that state can be a hair-shirt and the poet wears his with clinker gussets. Most people amble about the earth with their wits dim and their wicks well down, never likely to be ravished or startled by any apprehension of beauty or pity. They will be engaged in a kind of friendly rehearsal for death, and very nice it is for them. But for the poet vision and compassion are magnified to a point somewhere near the border of lunacy, if not well over and naturalised. He moves fluent as a fish through the enigmas of other people's lives. He is as conscious as a small jungle animal of the vast vitality that stirs and stalks through the patches of our self-willed darkness. W. H. Davies expresses this perfectly in 'The Hermit' who is moved

> When the moths on his night pillow beat
> Such heavy blows he fears they'll break his bones;
> Or when a mouse inside the papered walls
> Comes like a tiger crunching through the stones.

Often the poet in this state of delirious awareness realises that he can convey little of what he feels in ordinary language. T. S. Eliot would not at once be at ease with the Al Read characters who sound off on the bob bank, although their imagery might make bewildered contact at this point or that. The poet, therefore, often feels that he is a spy in a foreign land and he has to make his communications in the private code of a language so obscure that he himself, when correcting his proofs, feels that he is having to do with some kind of phosphorescent braille. But of W. H. Davies this could never be said. He was the plainest of poets. Most of his lines would have passed muster with the lovers of commercial television jingles. Take the most famous couplet that ever came from his pen:

> O what is life if, full of care,
> We have no time to stand and stare?

This has been trampled to such an extent by popular quotation each word of it is blue with bruising. If you quoted it today to a member of one of the more esoteric poetry groups he would either sue you or rush for the ammonia. But the whole of the matter is in those lines, the simple message that most of the lives led on this earth are bored, boring, brutish and wasteful; that in terms of active joy and ecstasy we do a considerably poorer deal than the average cow.

One cannot ponder the life of W. H. Davies with its gruesome seams of discomfort and humiliation without asking: Is a poet impelled to live in certain ways in order to become more of a poet? In the same way as a safe-breaker rubs his fingers with sand-paper in order to make them more responsive to the tumble and fall of the mechanism he has to crack, the poet has to rub his whole being raw the more easily to probe, shape and present the rich mysteries of being of which he wishes to be the spokesman.

I am reminded of a verse by one of the merrier gagmen of German mysticism, Gottfried Keller:

> Lo, I became a master to suffer and rejoice,
> And in the lust to suffer true ecstasy found voice.

I realise that this topic is capable of producing bigger clusters of nonsense than most others. But it can project a cooling air on some of the hottest bits of anguish in the human situation. Just take a second look at those lines by Keller. When they do the inescapable musical on schizophrenia, this is going to be one of the top lyrics. Chanted long enough it is going to extend the average split mind half-way down the back.

The lust to suffer is certainly plain in W. H. Davies. He bears out a belief I have always had that trouble dunked in tears is a sort of vitamin for most types of poetical impulse. Time and again in the story of verse you have the figure of the conscious poet walking into a strong gale of penury, self-abasement, exposed to every known type of shame and belittlement. Given the choice between latex foam and holly, the poet, at least for a short sit-down, would take holly.

Many of the great mystical poets of Spain practised the most scarifying austerities on themselves in order to obtain the blinding vision of the divine presence. Once, in Spain, I was told the tale of an all-out sixteenth-century mystic who had himself hung up by the right arm while he used the other to scribble songs of praise on the tonsure of a loyal colleague. This I discount. Yet a certain pressure of pain seems necessary to bring the poet the sense of strangeness of alienation from the average, to win an angle of sight that will pick out the traces of magical grace in our generally rather sombre and myopic experience.

The details of 'Super Tramp' are known to most. The early death of Davies' father caused the family's removal to the home of his grandfather, the sea-captain. 'When we were settled in private life our family consisted of grandfather, grandmother, an imbecile brother, a sister, myself, a maidservant, a dog, a cat, a parrot, a dove, and a canary bird. I remember those happy days and often wish I could speak into the ears of the dead the gratitude which was due to them in life, and so ill-returned.'

He was apprenticed to an ironmonger after a few incidents of inept thieving for which he was birched. His mind was soaked early in the sea tales of his grandfather. Poetry he loved and read from the start, and how this chimed with that birching we can easily imagine. He soon grew tired of the furniture trade on the fringe of which he was hammering the odd untidy tack into picture frames. On his grandfather's death he received an annuity which yielded him eight shillings a week. This pittance gave him a crazy illusion of the independence for which a poet lusts. In his late teens, by now totally anti-social, he went to America. No life can have had a less ambitious start. Arriving at New York he moved without a pause into a period of complete vagabondage. He knew what he wanted: nothing. And he went after it with both hands tied behind his back. No man could have moved with less fuss on to the outermost and most desolate rim of existence.

He found himself in gaol in the next cell to an American-Italian murderer. On leaving gaol he inquired of a compatriot of the felon how the trial had gone. The compatriot wanted to tell Davies that the prisoner had got life: 'Antonio, he no get part of de time, he get all of de time.' That is one of the very rare attempts by Davies to raise a smile. He must be one of the straightest faces to look out from literature. It is as if the laughter had been wrung right out of him.

For five years he 'rode the rods', risking death by a fall or a punitive roughing-up by railway guards. He learned the whole map of human gullibility, the thousand ways of wheedling a dime from the friendlier matron. He could coax a meal from a brick wall if the mortar were soft enough. Regular work he dodged as if it were bubonic. Then came the accident which cost him a leg. It was a misjudged jump on to a moving train.

If my theory of Davies's mental development holds water, the accident could have been half-deliberate. Men move dimly towards what in their essence they wish to become, and the things that happen to them have already been planted by them in the waiting darkness ahead. Davies wanted an end of his crass and futile loafing. From it, by normal means, there was no sensible issue. He had neither the money nor the training to effect a cool change of life. Only a broken body could have provided him with the spiritual drive that would take him away once and for all from the camp-fires of the hoboes and set him to forming the songs that must already have been loud and jostling in his head. Or, on the other hand, he might have just misjudged his jump on to that train; but it doesn't sound as good that way.

The period following his return from Canada stands as the most revolting of his life. The years of drifting in the U.S.A. had been bad enough but the land still contained enough space and ingrained anarchism to prevent the hobo from feeling the shabby dog he must feel in a society as stabilised and sniffy as ours. In London he stayed in a succession of hostels run by those curiously ambivalent people who seem to have as much hatred as love for the disengaged roamers to whom they give cheap shelter. Understandably, for social derelicts, at close quarters, can be an exasperating crew.

In this period Davies often came close to death as he sat in the collective 'living-room' of his current doss-house, in air drained as effectively of oxygen as of hope. He made frequent appearances before the officials of a charity organisation that existed to provide artificial limbs for paupers; or rather to withhold them, according to Davies, who was convinced that these smug little Pilates suspected that he was keeping a perfectly good second leg at home just to fool their committee.

In the meantime he wrote his lyrics, starved, begged, sold laces and matches around the doors to find the few shillings to get the poems printed, then hawked the broadsheets from street to street. Altogether as comprehensive a version of hell as can befall a sensitive and intelligent human, confirmation of the view that the life of Davies is best understood in terms of a self-inflicted cruelty aimed at preparing the spirit for a unique act of expression.

Then came the volume of poems which he sent to the eminent and the charitable. His lightnings flickered in a most dubious night. One copy reached Bernard Shaw. He gave the poet help and encouraged him to write *Super-Tramp*. Then came the years of mild celebrity, the friendship of many of the great artists of his time. He rarely rose clearly above the penury line and one wonders what could have been the exact colour of his thoughts as he stood, this austere man who looked rather like Sitting Bull's Calvinistic uncle, Preaching Bull, in parties with intellectual grandees whose lives had never known a single whiff of the sulphurous privations that had been Davies's midden for twenty years.

There is one disquieting little incident he tells of Max Beerbohm, the saint (according to most sources) of a gentle urbanity. He and Davies were at a small party. The topic of Shaw's having helped Davies had cropped up. Beerbohm stepped back, stared at Davies and said, 'Might that not have been a case of helping a lame dog over a stile?' It would take real effort to think of anything more crass to say to a one-legged tramp who has just come limping back into social normality after as ripe a round of degradation as one can imagine. Max must have had more fox-hunting blood in him than he knew.

Davies's last years were spent in relative happiness and prosperity, his fame solidly established in his poems and autobiography. But we are left with a mystery at the core of this man's life. What was the force that kept him rising through squalor to become one of the most renowned interpreters of natural beauty the earth has known? He never lacked a fierce and solemn belief in his own genius. Given enough of that, for it is a kind of anaesthetic madness, a man will survive even such an experience as 'grimping', singing hymns in the street in a voice so sad and bad that when a penny is thrown at you it is meant seriously to connect and hurt. He was never free from this feeling that he could bring to life an enriching radiance; no indignity could ever spoil it. Within him there was a sea-wall of pride and a knife of cunning defying all the Philistines and regimenters who are:

> In full cry to bring me down,
> All greedy for my magic robe,
> All crazy for my burning crown.

He had genius and I can think of no one more coolly convinced of having it. 'Of course, we know well that nothing can be done for genius. Unfortunately nature does not mark him at birth, or we could soon put an end to him, and not only save the State work but, better still, save him from the cruel sport of fame.' Fame never did anything to Davies as cruel as the things he did with such lavish masochism to himself; so call it quits.

No man ever distilled a greater beauty from a stranger dish than did Davies. No man ever stood more squarely and proudly in the middle temple of ecstasy and grace:

> I stare at dewdrops till they close their eyes
> I stare at grass till all the world is green.

That any man should carry through his life intact a cup of such enchantment would be estimable; that W. H. Davies should have carried his, unflawed, through the patch of his scuffed and hurting days is a miracle, no less.

DYLAN THOMAS

In all the astonishing things that happened in the life and death of Dylan Thomas I suppose the most impressive was the reception given to the news of his going. I hardly think there has been an event in the last half-century that has created such a significant hush in the normally noisy conscience of the Welsh.

Extreme adulation and extreme contempt still thrust their clumsy feet through his poor dust. Just to be in the act I would like to put forward a compassionate toe.

The poet, at the heart of whose being is a wish for peace, never really finds it. Fifty years from now Dylan will have entered a wilderness of academic appraisal. Our fifth and sixth forms will be faced with such questions as: Estimate the importance of D. Thomas as man and artist.

The first part of the question is easy. He created, from the muffled delirium in which most of a poet's days are bound to be spent, a universe of images from which each of us can draw some new illumination of insight and pity. As a man, when the storm of gossip has died away, there will emerge from his existence an impression of bewildered sadness that is present even in his moments of more deliberate buffoonery.

The poet carries the load of all our stricken and mutilated lives, and seeks, through intensity of expression, to bring restitution to those who have been too cruelly denied the gifts of beauty, wisdom and dignity.

In my copy of Dylan's collected poems are two portraits of him. One is the radiant youth painted by Augustus John, a handsome paladin across whose confidence and strength no shadow had yet fallen. The other picture was published in a magazine. It was taken just before his last journey to America. The face is of a man conscious of all the world's setting suns. The eyes are big, sad, death-charged and wise almost beyond reason.

But it is Dylan as a folk-figure, a piece of twentieth-century Welsh mythology, who remains most fascinating to me. He was a sort of living revenge on all the restrictions and respectabilities that have come near to choking the life out of the Welsh mind. In a land where so much of a man's work has been of a most wanton ugliness, he dedicated his life to an interpretation of beauty.

At a time when in South Wales alone a whole generation had their lives outraged by a monstrous, State-regimented poverty, he lived with a rebellious abandon that made the rest of us look like sullen convicts. That, I am sure, is why tens of thousands who had never read a line of his verse or even heard the radio pieces, felt that part of their own dream had been projected through him. In the midst of so much squalid and unprofitable labour, he lived on his own margin of nimble wizardry.

For those who feel that they might have dissipated some precious juice of artistry in a lifetime of loyal, family-bound drudgery, he gave the example of a quite ruthless insistence on dragging up from beneath the most stubborn silence the pattern of words he was born to create. For the shy and tongue-tied his voice was the brazen trumpet for which they long.

I can imagine some of the brickbats of violent contradiction that might be patted into shape here. I can see some of those who regret the passing of old ways and who believe that joy should be kept on a rigid leash. I can hear them say that Dylan's life was untidy, immoderate and self-destructive. True, there might have been elements of excess in his life. And the critics have been quick to point out Welsh poets who turned out work of the highest class while accepting the strait-jacket of civic normality and doing ordinary jobs.

The critics will hint at patches of what they consider a diabolic indiscipline in the life of Dylan Thomas, and say they will not hear of such a man being admitted as one of the folk-heroes of their day. Others will try to play down his achievement as an artist by saying that he only sprang to prominence because the English bourgeoisie, tired of hearing Welsh Radicals and Socialists saying critical and even menacing things to them in too clear a tone, welcomed him because he was the one Celt who would strike most people as talking the flattest and least scrutable sort of nonsense.

These people don't quite get the point. They can pile up a dossier sky-high to prove that, by their standards, Dylan might have been an impostor and nuisance. The truth is that facts play very little part in the moods and convictions of a community.

Dylan, in his strange, capricious way, represented for a mass of young Welsh people a dramatic moment in the restoration of joy to a people who for years had taken their religious sanctions too grimly and their pleasures too grossly. During the early years of this century the chapels on the one hand and the pubs on the other drew the opposing multitudes unto themselves. There was too little common ground between for that great body of people who feel that there is a place in life for contemplative reverence as well as for a flexible and worldly pursuit of delight.

Dylan Thomas was a protagonist of both. He expressed his love in ways and words that were often unintelligible to those who cling too

95

cautiously to the values and standards of the past. But the essence, the flavour he left behind will help us vitally in fashioning the idiom for a new social philosophy. In his own way he was a pulse-beat in the process of shaking off the cramping fears that had come to us from the social nightmares of yesteryear.

In his life there is a social tragi-comedy of the first class. His father was a teacher of English, a not very happy or successful one, I understand. The part of the teacher in the Welsh myth is a very important one and it has created some of the most interesting toxins. Our classrooms reek of dead and wasted talents.

For the last forty years of the nineteenth century the average life of the men who worked in pits, steel-works or farms was so base and discouraging that any father with a tittle of literacy to his credit dreamed only of putting his sons into jobs that would not dirty the hands, break the back or degrade the mind.

Teaching was the trade that involved the fewest philosophic or financial traps. So it was that shoals of our brightest minds drifted into a profession that holds more opportunities for static misery than most others. For a few garrulous exhibitionists and brazen egomaniacs it can be a tolerable and even pleasant job. Theirs is the Kingdom of Heaven, for they are sustained by the illusion that the young have a besotted affection for them. They will be convinced that, in front of a class, they have found the exact point of balance between majesty and buffoonery. They are the only kings with their own inbuilt clowns.

But for the teacher who is shy, recessive, inarticulate, teaching can be the plainest sort of hell. He senses and dreads a fermenting insolence in the young. He is normally frustrated by headmasters, worthy fellows most of them, but doomed by a total lack of creative gifts to see their function as a muffler on any bell of gaiety or sophistication. Or he will be hectored by inspectors, proud men with pricking tongues, slightly demented by the good fortune of having been able to dodge betimes out of the actual labour of teaching.

So the teacher of today is, so to say, in exactly the same place his father was a generation ago. At the coal-face, right at the hub of darkness and lacerations. He dreams of a world for his son in which he will inherit a new dimension of dignity and freedom.

In the case of Dylan's father it is doubtful if the vision he nourished for his son's life would have been outside teaching. He belonged to a generation that still viewed the clean security of school work as the golden ideal. His dream would have been of a brilliant academic career with the cherry of a headmastership or an inspectorship to top it. A life of potential authority with no room for humiliations and boredom. No dream ever slipped so disastrously through the floorboards. If there were a method of denying a child the dancing, destructive flame of genius, I wonder how many parents would use it.

Dylan, with not a single academic medal in his lapel, fled early from the school in which his father taught. He dickered for a while with local journalism and then, for the rest of his life, turned the most decisive back in Welsh history on diligence, convention and thrift, his mind torn from end to end with the labour of his astonishing verse.

In the last years, when he was falling apart under the weight of his own legend, his father must have looked at him with the grey-eyed amazement of the stricken Faustus, trying to find resemblances to himself in the demonic force he had conjured up from the sea of his own incurable yearnings.

97

Laugharne

HUW MENAI

Huw Menai, who died in 1961, was born in Anglesey. Physically, he was one of the most impressive men of his time. He was tall, handsome with the air of a sad conqueror, a king irretrievably betrayed. Of the three poets we are talking about he was the one most trapped by time and circumstance.

He came down from the north with the flood of landworkers seeking better wages in the mines. He was a pit-sinker, one of the men who actually made the hole that led down to the seams. The pit-sinkers were a kind of elite, strong, tough and mobile. They belonged to the great army of 'navigation men', the navvies who dug the canals, made the docks and laid the railroads that gave economic coherence to the last century. They were undomesticated, given to hard drinking and furious fighting. In moods of Saturday-night orgy the police left them to their bloody devices.

One sensed these origins in Huw, the sense of exile from the mountains of the north, the sense of having lived with violence and danger, and of having failed even in poetry to find an adequate replacement for them.

He worked as a boy in the Morfa colliery at Margam. It was an enterprise that ran under the sea. An explosion in the early years of this century burned to death and drowned several hundreds of men. Huw had a story about it. It was a terrifying tale, and Huw's style of delivery, slow, with his North-Welsh accent becoming more and more guttural, giving it an extra edge of horror.

After the charred bodies were brought up they were placed in a stable, laid out to await identification. Huw, a lad, was given the job of looking after the place. He stood by the door looking out to the sea and trying not to feel that the world's whole doom was on his shoulder. From behind him he heard a curious, rustling sound. He looked around, 'the slowest thing I have ever done with this head of mine'. One of the bodies had raised itself into a sitting position. It opened its eye, uttered the single word 'Mam!' and fell back, finally dead. 'And my insight into the nature, the texture of human life,' said Huw, 'deepened by a mile at that moment.'

During his youth he was an Anarcho-Syndicalist, the political sect that spread like a bush-fire in places as separate as Australia, California and the Rhondda. When Keir Hardie came to fight his first parliamentary battles in Glamorgan, Huw was one of his most passionate gonfaloniers. Hardie, short, impetuous, had a deep affection for the young man, and, so Huw said, at the end of a campaign, would call the tall young warrior to him, lay his hands on his shoulders and bring Huw's incomparable head to a level at which he could kiss his brow.

He married and had ten children. His wife, Anne, is as sweet and gracious a lady as will ever be bred in this land. He became unemployed early in the slump and the framework of poverty around his life settled into a classic rigidity.

What sort of poetry was likely to arise from such a life as this? The elements from which it was fused were simple and, in the end, deadly to the true expression of his talent. There was the Utopian, fervid socialism that did not grow a whit cooler for all the passing of the years and the rotting of dreams. To the last, in any paper that would print them, his letters spoke the good word for mankind, urging a sane and cordial resolution of our lusty dilemmas.

This is not good for poetry. The poet, to find the unique note that will contain all the vibrations of his spirit, needs to be fastidious, and to be fastidious one needs to be more than a little reactionary. A chilly contempt for man, from Shakespeare to Eliot, would seem to be a great refiner and sharpener of verse. Evangelical fervour, which was Huw's idiom (a generation earlier he would have been one of the great preachers), demands eloquence, turgidity, slackness, and each of these is a morgue for the muse. There is enormous power in much of his poetry. Indeed, in the early 1920's and early '30's, English critics found something Whitmanesque and admirable in the great splurge of proletarian protest and yearning which he expressed. For a short period he became almost as much of a cult as Dylan was later to become among some of the most refined literary cabals of the time.

But Huw was unamenable to that sort of world. He was stuck in his poverty, his family, his class, his stupid, irremediable time. In W. H. Davies and in Dylan there was an element of the picaro, the nimble-footed courtier who could always be counted on to produce a pleasing effect on the mighty. In Huw there was always a cloud of sad, serious awareness of our collective mutilation. His was the entire face of a harassed mankind. He would very shortly have depressed Dame Edith Sitwell.

Poverty can often provide the poet with a nerve. But it must be either the knavish, impudent poverty of a Villon or the total, death-like poverty of a Jack Clemo. Huw's was the foul, regimented poverty of a workless man in a state that had achieved the threshold of decency, far enough into a civilised ethic not to want to hang its sturdy vagabonds and sufficiently afraid of a more or less literate and organised plebs not to want to starve them.

The poles of his life for a long period were the mountain-top and the dole office. He was disliked by the pious as a freewheeling agnostic, detested by the less aware for his air of aristocratic aloofness. Poverty of that sort would have exhausted even Baudelaire's gift of disgust. The Rhondda valley was Huw's perfect seed-plot and perfect grave. There was no escape, no alternative. I cannot imagine him living anywhere else. He was born to keep success at a fair distance. Even when a band of devoted friends managed to gain for him a small Civil List pension, it came too late to give him any real pleasure or pride.

He spoke Welsh but did not write in it. His average attitude towards the chauvinists was one of melancholy impatience. Philosophically he never aimed lower than at the ardent internationalism that had filled his early years. He would never have accepted a view of life that dropped down dead at Chepstow. When some fanatical separatist told him that the Welsh language was the 'tongue of paradise' Huw's look suggested that he had always expected the worst of paradise.

He read enormously. There never were such readers as the men of that generation. They consumed print as if they believed that beyond a certain point of literacy they would achieve some saving radiance in them and the world. In Huw's case there was, in addition, a creative power that needed to be fed and shaped. He never managed to submit his talent to a correct discipline. He never found the word-gauge that infallibly warns some poets from a bad line. If a prolonged formal education does nothing else it gives the mind a sort of shyness that induces either a perfect sensitivity to words, or it induces silence, the conviction that nothing can ever again be said better than it has been said before.

I recall being asked to take part in a radio programme with Huw. The idea was that Huw be allowed to talk for half an hour with myself guiding the monologue into fresh paths if Huw tended to become too monotonously bardic. The few things I managed to say were excised from the tape and all that remained of me at the end were a few assenting grunts. I was referred to in a programme as an 'invaluable catalyst'. But Huw was great. He rumbled and glittered like an electric storm.

We did the recording at his home, in the 'front room'. It was a cold night. Huw's wife kept bringing coal into the room. Next door some bandsman was practising an everlasting trill on his oboe. On the recording the clink of the scuttle and the cooing of the oboe provided a weird

sort of obbligato to Huw's vatic flow. 'I stand on the hilltop. I stare at a
cloud. I feel a clean wind on my face. I hear a chit-chat talk to me from a
cranny in the wall. My whole being is charged with a sense of absolution
and renewal. Then my bowels are moved. The voice of the chit-chat
always seems to have this effect. I come down bowed beneath the vast
and terrible weight of my common humanity.'

In that mood Huw could be a master of majestic banalities. He was
talking about a long poem he had written. It was, I think, called 'Caleb
of the Slag Heaps'. One line of it was, 'I am but a maggot in a cheese of
chance.' Huw could not only take the bull by the horns, he could make it
rhyme as well.

One other echoing absurdity of that radio encounter arose out of
Huw's account of his attending an international conference of anarchists
in Dublin. 'I was idling along the banks of the Liffey, pondering the
problems of obscurantism and booze. A meek, swarthy man came up to
me and started to talk to me in a language I did not know. I spoke to
him in English. And as we talked non-stop and in loud voices we got
along well, and with no sense of anomaly. This man later abandoned the
doctrines of Anarchism totally. His name was Benito Mussolini.' A
secretary in the transcription department of the London B.B.C. was
puzzled by Huw's thick, North-Welsh accent. She could not see how the
Italian leader could have got into so clearly Celtic an act. In her final
version the dictator emerged as 'Benny Thomas Olliney'.

Huw was a man who could control great drifts of words. He could use
silence as well. In his last years he did a lot of lecturing on subjects like the
soul and destiny of man. His style was discursive and unbearably allusive
to people who had covered nothing like Huw's vast prairie of reading.
Buddha, Thomas Aquinas, Duns Scotus, Dante, Gandhi, Dr William
Price of Llantrisant. He would use them all as familiarly as if he had met
them that afternoon in Penygraig square. If you had said anything at all
it was hard to get left out of Huw's thesis. He tried to switch on the light
in the darkest rooms of moral philosophy.

The effect of lecturing on him was not good. During the last third of
his life his health was wretched. Very often, after about five minutes of
general introduction, he would fall quite silent, close his eyes and lay his
hands on his head. A greenish pallor would settle on his face. Then he
would say, 'You must bear with me. I felt strange on the bus down from
Penygraig, in the bus. Last week I also felt strange in the bus on the way
to Bargoed. There is something not at peace between me and movement.'
He would stay in this astral flight for as long as a minute. At the end of it,

without uneasiness or embarrassment, he would be back on the track of Aquinas, Scotus and the rest.

He told me an astonishing story of an incident that happened when he was quite a small boy in Anglesey. He was travelling by trap with the fierce, frustrated wife of a neighbouring farmer. Suddenly the light was blotted out from his eyes. She had thrown her huge skirts over his head. When he finished the story he said, very, very softly, 'I have been a bugger of a man.'

He lived on the other side of the mountain from me. His greatest delight was to walk for hours along the fern-lined paths of the plateau. Our paths often crossed. But being inward and downward-looking we never exchanged a word until we met over a pint of ale in a Pontypridd inn. On his hilltop he was a gaunt, Wordsworthian figure. It is the way I see him best, the way I would wish to remember him longest.

7 A Thought for the Dragon

As the immediate past has become loathsome, a thing it is thought tactless to drag into the light as we top up our ale with a froth of light engineering affluence, the far, bloody past has taken on a second wind with the rise of the Nationalists.

This fascinates me. In my childhood a belief in the unity and brotherhood of man was as urgent and compelling a force as the gambling mania of today. When we sang, 'He comes to break oppression and set the captive free, To take away transgression and rule in equity', we meant just that. The blend of evangelism and Jacobinical socialism had a power which we felt sure could dynamite all foulness off the earth. We lifted our eyes unto the hills with such dedication the hills got jumpy.

We were not, in terms of nationality, a homogeneous people. Into the valleys had poured as many Englishmen as indigenous Welsh. The only binding things were indignity and deprivation. The Welsh language stood in the way of our fuller union and we made ruthless haste to destroy it. We nearly did.

The tide of our final Radical rapture has drained away. The revival of the Welsh language has witnessed the most drastic contraction of dreams in the history of weariness. Whereas we and our fathers stood squarely on the proposition that we should raise to full stature all the human refuse on this earth at whatever expense in hernias, the national brain now bulges with such projects as the need to deny Welsh rainwater to the Liverpool water-board, and a demand that the present limited education we now give to our children in English should be replaced by an even more limited education in Welsh. The Nationalists are the only political group in Wales in which it is possible to see clear evidence of fervour and hope. There is less drama in that sentence than meets the eye.

This fanatical racial memory can be very seductive and exciting, especially to a community that has fewer live theatres per thousand of population than any land south of the Arctic. Indeed, as my own middle age ripens towards a total inertia, I might fall in with it myself. There might be greater joy in moving east with the phantom hosts of Glyndwr than in twitching uneasily in the presence of the world's current crop of bully-boys. And if the whole lot of us were to march back to the fourteenth century it might cause an extra twinge of anxiety to our lawmakers as they launch into an age of larger space and shorter railways.

A large part of my childhood was dominated by as ripe a specimen of Welsh chauvinist as ever I met. His surname had a slightly English overtone and he preferred to be known by his given name, Caradoc. He wore a heavy moustache which we thought he had modelled on that of Lloyd George, but he told us that it was identical with that he had seen worn by Welsh nobles in a painting of the court of Howel Dda. He was a short man with a stoop. The stoop came from having spent many years walking up the Rhondda hills brooding about the English. A part of it was due to his having worked briefly in his young manhood for a Welsh milkman in London, and this milkman had loaded Caradoc with his longest round and his heaviest churns. Had the milk not been somewhat lightened by dilution Caradoc was convinced he would have wound up armless in some Potter's Field near Ealing. For the milkman Caradoc felt no hatred. The poverty of the nineteenth-century Welsh peasant justified all the curmudgeonly antics of their emigrant brethren.

At least once a week, for as long as he was our teacher in the primary school, Caradoc would desert the simpler disciplines of the class-room and give us a summary of Wales's bloody past and threatening present. Like Hitler's treatment of the post-Versailles iniquities, the thing never seemed to lose its freshness. And he never started the story at a point later than its very beginning.

He would start with the 'mound-dwellers' who spent most of their time hiding, with every reason for so doing. The theme of hiding was a strong one in the mythology of Caradoc. Time and again, after describing some crisis of terror that had clipped the Welsh, he would picture them as sitting very quietly in caves and fox-holes until it was safe to try their luck again. To underline this point Caradoc would sink down in the hollow of his desk and crouch there for minutes on end, not saying a word. He suggested the dilemma of a shocked and recessed nation, and made us wonder whether we were not exposing ourselves unduly.

Then came the Ivernians who used slings, went naked into battle, painted their faces blue and built Stonehenge. Caradoc explained how the Ivernians got the great blue-stone monoliths from North Pembroke-shire to Salisbury Plain. His tongue would slither over this subject as if he were not too sure about it himself. We certainly were not convinced. Those blue faces, cheek by jowl with those blue stones had us confused. We never got close to the Ivernians.

Then came the Goidels and the Ivernians took to the caves. The Goidels were bronze-users and Caradoc held this against them. He made it clear that he favoured the Ivernians as he favoured the pre-industrial hillside-shepherds of our valley region. He also hinted that the Ivernians might have stood a better chance against the Goidels, bronze and all, if they had gone into battle clothed, and quarried the stone for their stone temples locally instead of lugging the stuff all the way from the Preseli mountains in Pembrokeshire.

'So don't forget. Fight fully clothed and use only local stone. And if your face is naturally white, let it show.'

Then came the Brython and the Goidels told the Ivernians to move up.

'In the darkness and the swamp the two defeated peoples forged a fierce, fighting unity that was to eventuate in the Welsh Rugby Union.'

When Caradoc came to the Romans his style became slower and more coherent. He made a production of the last battle of Caratacus. He did not give the great Silurian chief his British name, Caradoc, because he could see that since he bore that name himself we would be baffled. He explained to us about the *testudo*, the advance of the Romans beneath a virtual carapace of upraised shields. He got ten of us to fashion bijou shields of papiermâché. He himself would stand on a chair with a wooden sword, impersonating Caratacus and his beleaguered force. He did good work with this sword. He would shatter the shields and the lesson ended with first-aid being given to four or five stunned legionaries, while Caradoc intoned, 'I have shown you what it should have been like, had justice been done to the fire of Silurian pride.

'But in real life it was not like that. The *testudo* did its fell work. Roman blood flowed in rivers but the *testudo* did not break. Caratacus was betrayed by Cartismandua, wife of the King of the Brigantes, a woman of infamous record.' Caradoc was a bitter bachelor and if there was a woman of infamous record anywhere in the annals he would manage to bring her in. Caratacus was taken captive in chains to Rome.

And Caradoc would stand erect, stroking his moustache, faintly smiling. Then he looked the Roman Emperor right in the eye and made the speech that moved the Roman Senate to clemency. I think Caradoc made a bigger thing of this speech than did Caratacus. If the ancient Briton had carried on for as long as Caradoc the Senators would have had him thrown to the lions just to get back to their debauchery.

Very often the headmaster of the school, a distracted and silent man, would look in through a small window at these performances. But he did not interfere. There was a teacher shortage at the time and he had no wish to probe.

Caradoc could juggle with the genealogies of the ancient princes by the hour. 'Guitolion's grandson was the famous Gwrtheyrn Gwrthenen, or Vortigern of the Adverse Lips. This Vortigern was full of all sin and wickedness.' Caradoc would give us this news intensely, as if Vortigern were operating at that moment in the next street.

Then to Cunedda the Burner, who played hell with the Romans in North Britain. 'Cunedda was a Pict. There has been a lot of loose, libellous talk about the Pict. Ignore it. Cunedda was a Pict. Night after night, from their fortresses and their walls, the Romans looked at the reddening sky of their doom. Cunedda was at the torch again.' And Caradoc would move swiftly and ferociously among the desks simulating large-scale arson with an accuracy that brought the headmaster's eye to the little window. Caradoc would end this phase of the story thus. 'One day it will be proven that King Arthur the Peerless was really Cunedda the Burner and the Picts will come into their own again.'

He became gently lyrical about Saint David, 'the holy Dewi at whose passing the sun sank at noon and all humanity wept'. For years he promised us a trip to St David's Cathedral. 'I will show you the relics, the actual bones of this holiest of men who walked the earth in a dawn of goodness.'

We made the trip in a charabanc so old and unsprung it gave a medieval note to the whole pilgrimage. A fog started at Carmarthen and deepened by the minute. Caradoc put this down to the English who were out to baulk any effort by the Welsh to set eyes on the relics of their patron saint and scholar. By the time we reached the headland of Saint David about the only thing we could see was the gleaming starch of Caradoc's winged collar. We foxed various villagers by walking into their cottages demanding to be shown the relics.

Many incidents from the far past seemed to find a unique mouth in Caradoc. History glowed through him to the point where he ceased to be a teaching man in a brick school in a broken town and one saw only a skeleton of remembrance. He was very good on Gruffydd the Second, the prince who tried to keep afloat in the first wave of the Norman Conquest. He could recite the names of the first great border-barons as a kind of black and sour litany. Hugh the Wolf, the Norman Earl of Chester, Robert of Rhuddlan and the rest. Caradoc would often visit the castles at Ludlow, Chester, Ross, where the captive Celts were once treated to courses of fetters, hot oil, eye-gouging and worse.

'And worse. Nameless were the things those French and Saxon rogues did to our men and nameless they shall remain.'

This disappointed us for we had stomachs strong as brass for horror.

'Do not ever forget Meirion Goch, Meirion the Red. No, no, I do not mean Meirion Pugh the Anarcho-Syndicalist from Bedwas Road who is also called Meirion the Red. This Meirion I'm talking about has been dead for close on a thousand years, and not a day too short for my money. He was the rodney who betrayed Gruffydd into the hands of Hugo the Wolf, who was a friend of Robert of Rhuddlan. Gruffydd lay for six years in Chester, in chains, and the iron made a meal of his flesh. He was rescued by Cynric Hir, Cynric the Tall, a young chieftain who crossed the Dee with the lacerated Gruffydd on his back. For years Gruffydd wandered. You know the story of Moses, how for forty years he wandered. Gruffydd walked even further. More uphill. He was known as Gruffydd the Wanderer.'

There was a local man called Hughes the Totterer, an erratic, cider-drinking marathon walker whose face we conjured up at every mention of Gruffydd.

'Gryffydd raided the castle of Robert of Rhuddlan at Deganwy. They met face to face, Gruffydd and Robert. The Welshman won and he sailed away, his ship full of the Norman's sleek, black cattle and on the top of his mast . . . guess what?'

We all knew. But we'd make a few guesses just to stoke Caradoc's passion up a few degrees. 'A flag.' 'The Red Dragon rampant with pride.' 'The jerkin of a fallen foe.'

'No!' And Caradoc's smile would be devilish under his medieval moustache. 'Nailed to the mast was the head of Robert of Rhuddlan. I am against nailing, thinking it a crude and noisy tactic. A nice bit of quiet dove-tailing is the very summary of love as I see it. But on that occasion, there at far Deganwy, Gruffydd could have trusted me with the hammer.'

Places where blatant anti-Welsh treachery had happened were never, for Caradoc, quite disinfected. 'Take Abergavenny. Had many a charabanc outing to Abergavenny. Nice, pleasant, harmless-seeming place. Enjoyed it. But that was before I read about Iorwerth ab Owen. This took place in the reign of Henry the Second who was a knock to Becket and a serious nuisance to the Celt. Under a flag of truce Iorwerth came to visit the castle at Abergavenny, whose lord was William de Breos of Brecknock, and if you cannot hear villainy in that man's name you have not been getting my message. With Iorwerth to Abergavenny came Sesyll ap Dunwal and the rest of his kinsmen. De Breos had provided a feast and the dessert was hard and bitter. Around the banqueting hall were stationed a ring of butchers under the command of Ranulf Poer, the Sheriff of Hereford, and that's another place you can keep your eye on. Hereford. At a signal the Norman wolves ravened in and massacred the unarmed guests. So, don't forget, Abergavenny. Next time you go there and call in anywhere, say, for a cup of tea, keep your eyes wary and wide open. And whether you go there by bus or train, keep your fingers on your return ticket.'

Builth Wells was another place perpetually dark for Caradoc. It was near Builth, 'near the little church of Llanynys beside the dark Yrvon' that Llewellyn the Last was betrayed and slain. He would show us a coloured picture of the last prince, standing by the ford, his hair golden, a short, futile sword in hand, wearing a scarlet tunic and a blue cloak, and his face pained as an armoured knight puts a lance through his chest. It was a river-bank where broom grew in profusion. 'Go to the spot and the people will tell you that no broom has ever grown again in Llanganten parish from that dark day to this, not until recently anyway. I've tried to be fair to Builth. More than once I've cured various disorders of the lower bowels by taking heavy draughts of its harsh and purgative spa-water. I had been brooding about Llewellyn the Last and Builth's undoubted complicity in his death. I went into the pump-room. I took my usual heavy swig of the liberating stuff. My bowels did not stir. They probably thought, as I did, that it would have been treachery to the ghost of Llewellyn to react in the usual squalid way. I doubled the dose and the supervisor set two attendants to watch me and declared a state of emergency. A great eruptive grief filled me. I left the pump-room with the feeling that I was shortly going to fall apart. I walked to the stream-side spot where the great Llewellyn and the broom in which he stood both died. The Builth waters sprang like Normans to the kill. Any day now broom will grow again on that fell spot.'

Caradoc's trip through our bloody patch of national time ended with Owen Glyndwr. 'Blessed is he whose death in the minds of his compatriots is an end and a beginning. Listen!' He would put his head on one side and open his mouth wide to provide a kind of radar-trap for all the mysterious, elusive sounds that come out to us from the perished past. He would tell all of us to do the same. We did so. We tilted our heads and dropped our jaws excessively. To a passing eye, and the eye of our paranoid headmaster was never far from the tiny window that gave on to our classroom, we must have looked like the finest gallery of dolts ever organised.

'Listen. You will hear him as he passes furtively through the hills during those last, terrible years. Hunted, heartbroken, hurt in mind and body. There is no valley in the land through which he can pass without seeing or sensing the endless graves of comrades slain. He carried the death of a nation upon his back. He fashioned for his soul a unique torment. Is it any wonder then that he did not completely die, that he waits even now beneath a friendly and lightly poised rock for the moment of recall. He may be lying at Ogof y Ddinas, a cave well to the west of here, an area where the high wages in the anthracite industry and an obsession with Rugby football will have dropped Owen to the bottom of the agenda. The only real significance that Ogof y Ddinas has today is that from this cave is obtained some type of dust or powder which is used in the making of false teeth. This puts Owen into a poor light and marks one of the most serious declensions of glory even in our own jerky annals.

'But he'll be back. He'll be back to twit the local councillors on their failure to curb a rising rate, and end the scandal of that burning tip at the bottom of Bethesda Row which gives out flames and a smell evil enough to make the grave seem a wholesome proposition. He'll be back to censor Lloyd George for having allowed himself to become the pawn of warlords and for having extended needlessly the area of Welsh participation in world butchery. He'll be back to trip up the schemes of those clowns who want to shore up the walls and refill the moat of Caerphilly Castle, that badge of national disgrace, though I see that a brisker tourist trade to the restored fortress might offset the eclipse of the cheese trade in that area. The recurrent Owen would also have some blistering things to say about the Liberal-Labour faction whose utterances are doing so much to mist over the old simplicities.'

Years after we left the primary school we went to see Caradoc again. He lived alone. He was feeble and failing on almost every physical front. He sat, shawled and stooped, in front of an immense fire. His greeting as we came into the room was barely audible. Heat and melancholy seemed on the point of making the silence final. Caradoc's hand could be heard moving over his woollen covering, as if following the track of his mind as it groped back to the bridge that would bring him back to us. And we sought for the word, the name that would flick his passion alive again and bring him in the nick of time from under the falling dark. We took it in turns to sustain the fanfare of national remembrance.

'Caratacus.' 'Cunedda the Burner.' 'Meirion Meirionydd.' 'Rhodri Mawr.' 'Gruffydd the Wanderer.' 'Llewellyn the Last.'

He made no reply. Even his hand upon the woollen shawl fell quiet. No one stirred among the mountains and the light had drained away from all the hills.

We left the house.

8 Dusk and the Dialectic

THERE was a time when the Birchtown Institute was a very considerable place. The walls were distempered to match the prevailing shades of philosophic determinism. Acid overtones of radical dissent had eaten into the dark didactic murals. In the draughts room there was a plaque over the spot where Ramsay Macdonald had sat to play a game after being driven in by a cloudburst that had dispersed the open-air meeting he was holding in 1911. On the top of the main staircase was the photograph of a man who had shaken the hand of Gandhi.

At one time the lecture hall had boomed with orators, and thousands of members had developed a sort of eye-trouble known as 'magic lantern blink', brought on by too violently adjusting the eye-balls on hearing any sound similar to the rap of the pointer that introduced a change of slide. And Birchtown always seemed full of that type of sound. The smaller rooms of the Institute had been full of tight, intense classes of adult thinkers that had been going on for anything up to twenty years on topics ranging from the Seven Qualities of Godhead to the Fourteen Points of Wilson.

Now the lecture-room was silent and some climax of tedium and shabbiness had caused the last of the disputatious students to creep away from the smaller rooms. The rot had started with the anthropology class, the deepest-rooted comb in the whole thinking hive. One Thursday night they had suddenly stopped in mid-concept, feeling as old as the material they had been handling. And they had walked forth from the Institute renouncing all interest in man's beginnings. Their faces were blank, their eyes emptied of all the lighted curiosity of yesterday and their arms were anthropoidally adroop. Two of them had taken to Dadaism and the rest to drink.

Affairs of the Nation

Some wrestling bouts had been tentatively arranged in the lecture-room, but they had drawn only tiny audiences, and the heavier falls of the fighters had caused bits of ceiling to land on the head of the librarian who was already dazed by the swift eclipse of literacy in the Institute, and who was in no mood to put up with any more.

A residual life went on in the draughts- and chess-rooms, but the players sat for so long in a state of querulous stillness that it seemed they were merely trying to fox death. The snooker-room was the one section that still buzzed and glowed a little, but the clients there were torpid and thoughtless and when the door of the snooker-room was left open the eyebrows of the man who had shaken the hand of Gandhi were seen to grow lower and darker.

The youthful users of the snooker-room had organised a soccer team. It had been fairly successful. Its violent lack of finesse had taken it to the top of the league table and landed dozens of its opponents in bed or flight. The dwindling core of the Institute's older members regarded these athletes sadly, seemed to be pulling their togas around them more tightly against an evening wind every time they heard them talk, and referred to them as Goths. The players took this as a kind of compliment and would have taken the field as the Birchtown Goths had they not been already certified in the league's annals as the Birchtown Stormers.

A month ago it was decided that the Institute should close. I went along to pay my last regards. I was met at the door by the two men who have been virtually running the place for years past. They are brothers, Conrad and Leroy Cromwell. They are short, battered men who once fought at ten stone under the names of Kid and Trooper Cromwell. Con and Leroy do not now look pensive. They have faces like the walls of caves, but at one time they had come greatly under the influence of the various thinkers who had sat in the ante-rooms of the Institute. They would often carry something of the humanism they absorbed in the lectures into the ring. On their bath-robes, instead of their names, they would often have such slogans as 'War is Disease'. And Leroy, who wore a much longer bath-robe than Conrad, had sported, 'Crime is a Chemical Product, like Sugar'. This so worried the referee, who had not done so much reading at one go for months, that he wanted to disqualify Leroy before a blow was struck.

But the years had taken all that with them. The brothers had receded from the light faster than the light had of its own volition failed. Their interest was in the snooker-room which yielded an income and a sort of uncomplex companionship that recalled to them the friendly rigours of the ring.

Leroy doubled as librarian and had developed such a spite against print that he had practically paralysed that side of the Institute's life. He had once gone for two whole evenings frowning at clients who approached the shelves and running down literacy, and he had issued just one book, a volume on masochism to a man who was later picked up for tying himself into knots that the police described as sinister.

The brothers Cromwell and I walked around the Institute. They were quite happy as they showed me the bustling snooker-room. They had already bought up the four tables at firewood rates and were going to use them to set up a saloon in another part of the town.

We moved along the corridor. We came to a door on which was painted 'The Sam Arnell Room'. Sam Arnell had run a class on Ethics in the Institute for twenty years, and talked some of the most violently impulsive voters in the zone into the quietness of mice. The extreme Left had derided him as The Great Gelder, but Sam had weighed in with his weekly two hours of calm and toothless persuasion. His climax came when he addressed an audience composed entirely of amateur boxers and wrestlers on the topic, 'The Need for a Total Passivity'. After talking for sixty-two minutes he looked at their faces, saw the undented serenity of their conviction that not only was Sam barking up the wrong tree but might with profit be buried under it. Sam went home and never spoke another word outside the banalities that keep a man warm and fed.

We pushed open the door of The Sam Arnell Room. A thick smell of still air and dead words came forth from it. A solitary man was sitting on the bench nearest the dais. He did not turn around to see who we were. Some sorrow lay right down his back like a panther. His head was only inches away from his knee cap. I could see that the man had taken the whole dose. I looked closer and recognised him by his spectacles. We left the room and closed the door very softly, as if out of respect for the dead.

'That was Charlie Barlow,' I said. 'Why was Charlie all hunched up like that in that crypt?'

'You know Charlie,' said Leroy Cromwell. 'He's a great student. He's gone almost blind with study in a dark kitchen. His wife doesn't like the look of Charlie. So she keeps the kitchen dark and most of the books that Charlie loves have print that needs headlights to read. You can see the dust on Charlie's eyeballs. He never missed a single lecture given by Sam Arnell. And Sam promised that when he had finished his twenty-year course on Ethics in general, he would surrender the dais to

Charlie who would then give a series on the Ethos of Conflict in the South Wales Valleys. But when Sam finished, the class just vanished. We never saw Charlie after that until the day it was announced that the Institute was going to close for good. He came in and asked if he could go into The Sam Arnell Room. He was there a long time. We looked in, just to keep an eye on the property. There he was, his head flat down on the dais and crying his eyes out. Compared with the way he looked then, the way he looked tonight was laughing and dancing.'

'And he never got to give his lectures on conflict?'

'Oh, no. He had twelve prepared. We heard him muttering when we took him out for a few gills to get over his grief. Oh, no, he never gave them. There wasn't anybody to listen. Kind of thing just went out of date, I suppose. He'd have been talking to himself.'

We were standing under the photograph of the man who had shaken Gandhi's hand and, looking more closely at the inscription at the photograph's foot, I saw that this voter had also received a letter of thanks and greetings from Keir Hardie.

'You owe something to Charlie Barlow,' I said.

'What do you mean?' asked Leroy.

'Once this place was full of dreams. He tasted them just like you did. Give him a chance to give those twelve lectures he prepared years back.'

'Twelve lectures?' said Con, and in the way he said the word twelve you could hear Barlow's voice going on and on for ever.

'It would give the old place a fine last curtain,' I said.

'It would, too, I suppose. But who'd listen to Charlie Barlow? Charlie's no tonic. I've heard him.. I know. Between ourselves, it was a vote of thanks from Charlie that drove me and Conrad to boxing.'

'You two run this place. You can get him an audience.'

We went back to The Sam Arnell Room and told Charlie Barlow that from the next Tuesday evening he was to give his twelve lectures on the Ethos of Conflict in the South Wales Valleys. At first he was wary, hardly bothering to break the stooped and stricken posture in which we had first seen him. He stared at Conrad and Leroy Cromwell as if this offer was the kind of cruel joke he could expect from two ageing pugilists, the last mental act of the snooker-room before the demolition men moved in. I persuaded him that the offer was sincere and effective.

He was delighted. I asked him to go up on to the dais to test his voice. Through the years of his recession he had got into the habit of muttering, and Leroy and Conrad had to bend right over the dais to hear him, and we could not accommodate a whole audience in that way.

'Make it louder, Charlie, louder and livelier. And find us a sample of the kind of material we can expect, because we've got to sell this project to some pretty dense voters up there in the snooker-room.'

Charlie gave us a brisk account of a great-grandfather who in the first half of the last century had been a member of a primitive trade union group in Carmarthenshire. This group had a way of planting explosives beneath the houses of non-members. Charlie's great-grandfather had the job of storing the dynamite, and he had it planted beneath a rough convenience at the bottom of the garden. One evening a non-member had thrust a fuse into the store while the great-grandfather had been sitting immediately above it. When they found him they built a small memorial to his memory.

Con and Leroy nodded.

'That's the stuff. That'll please the boys, Charlie. Nothing too deep. Plenty of death, action and bangs. Fine.'

The following night I was with Con and Leroy when they began recruiting students in the snooker-room. The first reaction of the players was to threaten to pelt the brothers with snooker balls and let them have one with the cue. But Con and Leroy were solidly behind the project now and would not accept refusal. Charlie Barlow had been following them around as pathetically as a rewarded dog and they were not going to disappoint him.

They approached the captain of The Stormers, the soccer team that had been formed from the snooker-room. He was a hard and ferocious lad called Harold Fenton. He had given a new muscle of confidence to backwardness in the zone and he broke into a kind of shingles at the sight of a book.

'Now, look, Harold,' said Con. 'You'd better keep in with us, boy. When the effects of this place are sold up your team is going to get new kit and a hut for changing out of the proceeds. Think of that. A hut. Won't that be better than changing behind bushes?'

'Better than the bushes,' said Harold. 'But Barlow! For twelve weeks.'

'You'll be amazed when you start to listen. Better than a Western. And don't forget that when we get that new saloon you are in line to become deputy manager.'

Harold came as near as he could to a nod of understanding, and hinted that with violence, gifts of beads and hand signals, he would work upon his friends.

Leroy had a good look at Harold's friends as they leaned over the tables or lolled on the benches.

'The best thing would be not to tell them anything in advance. Just get them into The Sam Arnell Room next Tuesday and leave the rest to us and the magic of Charlie.'

On the Tuesday night I saw Charlie Barlow approaching the portals of the Institute a good half-hour before the starting time of his lecture. He was carrying a vast wad of papers, baled and trussed as if for sale as waste. He was bent double and gasping badly over it. Leroy Cromwell came to join me on the steps of the Institute.

'What are you up to, Barlow?' he asked. 'Moving?'

'These are my notes.'

'You mean you are going to read all those documents tonight?' Leroy's upraised arm was already half dismissive.

'No, no. Not all tonight. I just wanted to give the boys an idea of the research that's gone into this theme.'

'It'll do that. You've dug up a lot of stuff there.' Leroy was peering into the bundle of notes as if expecting to find parts of Charlie's great-grandfather there.

We helped Charlie get his load on to the table of The Sam Arnell Room. He sat down and vanished from sight behind the mountain of manuscript.

'You'd better select the notes you want and shove the rest into a corner. It'll baffle the boys to see just that pile of stuff and no trace of you.'

'No, no. I want them to have a clear idea of the labours that have gone into this particular fight for the truth. It'll teach them a new respect for the lust to know that was Sam Arnell's greatest attribute.'

'All right then,' said Con Cromwell, who had just joined us and was circling the mound of notes, touching them gently as if proving to himself that they were there. 'But I think you're pitching the note too high, Charlie. Come on, Leroy. Let's get the audience.'

Then began the worst half-hour of my life. Word of Charlie Barlow's twelve weeks' course of lectures had by now filtered down to the last bedrock of snooker players, and they had quite bluntly tipped Harold Fenton the black spot. When I went into the snooker-room the players were huddled into a corner being harangued by Con and Leroy with Harold Fenton behind them, his fists held up in a generally threatening way.

'Rather than sit at the feet of Charlie Barlow, I'd swallow a set of snooker balls,' said Elphin Bragg, one of the players. 'Once I heard him. My arm was broken and he trapped me in a corner. He talked to me about the Sankey Award. I had to gum my ears back on by the time he finished.'

'He was related to Sankey, and he tended to go on about the Award.'

'You'll have to tie me down,' said another of the players, and Leroy sent for some rope.

'This is a kind of funeral for the Institute,' said Con, 'and you rodneys will fall in respectfully and march if it's the last thing you do.' He turned to me. 'Go down to Charlie and tell him his audience is on the way.'

I made for the door as Con laid his tremendous arms on the voter who had said he had heard Charlie talk about the Sankey Award. Con hustled Bragg to the door where Harold Fenton was stationed. Harold took a firm hold of Bragg and threw him without any waiting down the stairs. As Bragg landed and picked himself up Leroy Cromwell gathered him in a kind of Rugby tackle and literally tipped him into The Sam Arnell Room.

Charlie Barlow poked his head around his notes and said, 'Good evening, friend,' as Elphin Bragg came hurtling into the room. 'There's no need to hurry. There'll be plenty of room, I expect.' Before Elphin could see who was talking to him Charlie's head had vanished once again behind the notes, but this did not seem to worry Elphin. He got to his feet and with an angry roar bolted for the door. He was met by Leroy who sent him shooting back into the room.

Charlie said, 'Good night, friend,' again. Then the rest of the audience came landing on the room like shells. They were forced into position on the first two benches. The brothers Cromwell and Harold Fenton stood by the door and just nodded their heads at anyone who moved or made any gesture of wishing to withdraw.

'Fire away, Mr Barlow,' said Leroy, and several of the snooker players who had been clouted especially hard on their journey down the stairs looked astonished when Charlie came into view behind his tumulus of prepared material.

Charlie began. He explained that his first lecture, while concerned with some stirring physical events, could only be understood in full in the light of certain philosophical propositions. He then started one of the slowest strolls on record around the prison yard of the dialectic. Harold Fenton went into a mental sleep just one leaf of darkness away from death. Four of the snooker players began a distraught humming. Con and Leroy Cromwell leaned forward trying to find a chink of light in the gloom.

'Karl Marx,' said Charlie, thinking it wise to introduce a big name here if only as a challenge to the humming which was growing louder. 'Karl Marx found the idealist Hegel on his head, and in the interests of a humanist materialism just put him on his feet.'

'This is better,' said Con. 'German acrobats now.'

Then the line went dead again as Charlie walked serenely into a thicket of references to the mutative leaps set off by increases of size and numbers. He complicated this by referring to an article he had recently read in a *Digest* about air being electrified above certain points of speed. He even nipped into some side alley where he discussed what might happen to fruit if the fruit fly were given its head, but he told us that we would probably get a clearer picture if we ignored this.

The four distraught hummers gave up. They stopped singing, started roaring with laughter that was seamed with lunacy, and made a break for the door. The three guardians had all the work in the world getting the rebels back to the front benches.

'Give us a chance, Barlow,' shouted Leroy. 'Give the boys something to bite on. Give them some of that homely stuff about the man in the refuge who was blown up.'

'No, no,' said Charlie. 'Sam Arnell would have wanted me to be thorough, he would have wanted the basic premises clean and tidy.'

And on he went. The humming was resumed over a wider area, and Elphin Bragg was drawing up a long list of old favourites he wanted to hear before Charlie ran out of air. The snooker players were walking about playing with the window cords. They were not rebuked by the Cromwell brothers who were now slumped on a bench alongside Harold Fenton. Harold had eased himself into a sleeping position. Even I felt as if I had been at the opium.

Charlie's bliss of exposition must have taken about twenty minutes to lose its bloom and resume its contact with the bruising air. He raised his eyes from the stack of notes. He became aware that lyrics were now being hung on the humming. He began studying one by one the in-different, hostile faces. He tried a smile which got lost at once in sucking sand.

'Friends,' he said, 'it daunts me to see you all looking so distant. I wish I could have been like you, right from the beginning. But I won't keep you from your laughter, your fun.'

He picked up his notes. A great sheaf of them slipped away from the main load and fell to the ground. The mood of the room changed. Pity rose like a quick wind.

'Oh, no, Mr Barlow.' They were all up on the dais helping Charlie to find his scattered documents. I saw Elphin Bragg push a few pages into an inside pocket and urge a few companions to do the same, but in the main their charity was pure.

'Oh, no, Mr Barlow. Carry on, boy. We are for you. Let it rip, Charlie. This is good stuff, honest now. Snooker's no answer to daftness nor soccer an answer to death.'

They resumed their places eagerly on the benches.

But Charlie lifted his notes and walked slowly away from the room.

'Don't anybody come with me,' he said as he saw us rising. 'Stay in here until I've left the building. That's all I ask of you.'

Half a minute later we heard the front door bang. The snooker players rushed back to their games. There was no sign of Charlie. He had gone and with him he had taken the photograph of the man who had shaken hands with Gandhi and got a letter from Keir Hardie.

9 Devotions

To anyone who has known a country like Spain where you have a profound imposed religious unity, the brittle spiritual body of a place like Wales is a thing to wonder at. If the theological vigour of even fifty years ago had kept its impetus, the denominational ratio would by now be running somewhere in the region of one sect per man. Such a rage to dispute and divide must have pointed to some fundamental wish to reject the whole doctrine of revelation.

The chapels filled our early lives. Culturally and educationally they competed with the State schools. The Sunday school that I attended was as rugged a battlefield as the Somme. The social environment, based on an industry in which you stood an even chance of either moving up with an explosion or out with a slump, gave little encouragement to humility and modesty. The kind of dozy acceptance preached by the Established Church we would have rejected with the sharp ferocity of a peasant's pitchfork. As children we tended to regard the English Church as the recruiting ground of blackleg labour in the disputes that shook the place periodically like earthquakes.

And within the chapels themselves there was endless ferment. Fundamentalism and a neurotic unease about the desires and antics of the flesh had made any sort of suavity impossible. In the average congregation the local pit owner or manager was the king. His deacons would normally be the deputies and overmen and firemen who ran his pit. The preacher he would expect to be servile to his own little quirks of doctrine in religion and politics. If the preacher turned out to be a runaway independent with enough power of intrigue or eloquence to turn the larger part of the congregation against their master, then the latter would stamp out, followed by his little court, and found a new conventicle near by. New chapels flew through the air like shrapnel. In the

street where I grew up there were dozens. There were two of the same denomination frowning at each other across a narrow street. It was little wonder that when poverty and disbelief ravaged the valleys the chapels emptied like tube-stations after a raid.

The pressures in the Sunday school were enormous. Our denomination was Congregationalism, the most libertarian and humanistic of all the branches of Dissent. Ritual and ornamentation were whittled down to nearly nothing. If one saw a neighbour bending low in his pew it scarcely ever meant more than that he was fiddling with his bowler. A deacon who turned out with a chrysanthemum in his lapel was ticked off for being subversively rococo. It was a kind of Last Chance Saloon before one entered the Petrified Forest of rejections.

In the Library and Institute an artillery park of irreligion boomed, and we, the young of that time and place, were the finest sort of echoes that that type of explosion will ever wish to hear. If you heard an exceptional racket in that place they were either making an extension to the snooker-room or smashing ikons. We forswore hope for the individual on earth and beyond in favour of a belief in corporate bodies. If we looked up into the night sky we were not terrified of the silence of endless space. We were sure that it would become more voluble when the basic facts of brotherhood started to work to an inter-galactic programme. We believed that the Council laid on the stars and that they would become brighter when we had a more emphatic swing to the Left. When adolescence and its regal eagles of new desires came along we had no doubt that it was merely a significant bonus from the Miners' Federation.

The language of the chapels was, of course, Welsh, which we did not know. I might have muttered a few words of it in the shawl but as soon as I hit the anglicised air of the streets, even those few sounds vanished. But there was no question of our being withdrawn from the Welsh chapel and made affiliates of a place where we would have a fighting chance of getting the message. While my father, in middle life, batted broadly on the same wicket as Bradlaugh and the other sceptics, he retained a residual piety which strengthened as he grew older, back into a desperate kind of orthodoxy.

There we stayed, the captive and virtually deaf audience of veteran divines who considered that no worth-while point could be made in less than sixty to ninety minutes. In the tundra of boredom we devised bleak little games. We had one that concerned visiting preachers. There were many of these, for the chapel finances got rougher with every year, and when there was not enough to find the stipend of a resident pastor the call went out to any preacher who had a free Sunday.

We made a study of these peripatetic prophets. We would listen to them carefully as they announced the first hymns and did the readings, and we would gauge their oratorical scope. Then, just before the sermon, we went into action. We had all provided ourselves with twopennyworth of the same brand of toffees, in those days a fair load. We would contribute two toffees each to a common pool. Then we would wager that the preacher would be an eight-toffee, a nine-toffee man or what have you. And the one who was on that particular toffee when the sermon stopped would scoop the pool.

Sometimes the preacher, excited by the responses of a new audience, would still be speaking when we no longer had anything to chew. When that happened we simply had to sit there, trying from his gestures to figure the preacher's drift, and rustling the toffee-papers partly to torment the sidesmen, who loathed us, partly to beat back the onset of diabetic coma after that massive intake of sugar. This meant that by the time we were ten we were theologically as virginal as any dog. But this did not mean that we stood completely outside the verbal traffic of the chapel.

My brothers and I were forced to memorise in Welsh some of the longest and most passionate moral homilies ever composed. From the age of seven onwards we were putting such a knock on drink and adultery, you could almost hear thirst having second thoughts, and we put a stammer into the Welsh libido which it still has not wholly lost. Hillside lovers would go and look for wild flowers, between bouts of affection, in case the sensual impulse should get overtly out of hand. Even today we can go into pubs frequented by noted lechers of an earlier generation, and as soon as they see us they put down their glasses and go home, thoughtful.

Collecting funds for missionary work was a prime strand in our fabric. This puzzled us. With so many splendid examples of breakdown and dereliction in front of our eyes, a society barely a half-century old and already vitiated by every known disunity of the flesh and spirit, we thought it excessively obliging of the deacons and the ladies of the Zenana League to worry so much about the illiterate and sick of all the world's slums. Often one would see mocking groups forming at odd corners and making unChristian noises in the hope of attracting a missionary.

Week after week in the chapel came the stream of appeals for the work the missionaries were doing in the fight against nescience, yaws, nakedness and the other stigmata of an unbaptised condition. If our enthusiasm ever grew chill, we were told the story of Seithenyn Pugh, a local boy who went as a missionary to Papua. He dived apostolically into the deep end of the terrain and he was eaten. We were told privately that Pugh had always been feckless. Our informants were the lads who sat nightly in the lecture-rooms of the Institute, stroking Schopenhauer and praising a local man called Chepstow Ellis who had a way, on

The Road to the Chapel

Saturday nights, of standing alongside the Salvation Army Band on the square demanding to be struck by an avenging bolt if there were still a God interested in vengeance.

Ellis was never struck by a bolt but he was hit spinning by the bass-drummer, a new convert and a man whose veneer of tolerance refused to take the strain under the pitiless rain of provocation from Ellis. But it was a hard enough clout to convince Ellis that it might have been some kind of supernatural judgment, and after that he played it safe by just standing near the band, mainly silent and opening his mouth only to criticise brass band music in general.

Theoretically our work for the missionaries enriched us greatly. Several times a year we were put on stages to perform playlets that put in a strong word for spreading the faith into the earth's dark corners. Several of us, who had faces of a brutally fierce or contumacious kind, were picked to play the parts of natives hostile to the missionaries, besotted by pagan rites and only prevented from firing the mission house by inertia or beri-beri, or poor methods of arson. I was usually the leader of this faction. I had a loud voice and quick hands, and at the first sight of the missionary I would go into a harangue based closely on the style of one of our local Labour leaders, the only real difference being that when the local Labour leader spoke he was fully clad and I would be half-naked and have my body darkened by burned cork.

I would urge my fellows to treat the missionary either with indifference or the keen practical appetite that had made such short work of Seithenyn Pugh. The missionary would treat me with love and forebearance. Then I would be struck down by a falling tree, sleeping sickness, or savaged by the witch-doctor, a clumsy tactician, who wanted to blame the assault on the missionary. They had a dozen doses of doom meant just for me. But the missionary could circumvent the lot and the playlet would end with me at prayer and decently clothed. In the course of these shows I spun from one socially subnormal area to another at such a speed that, coming on top of the basic Welsh-English confusion, I felt and still do feel as multinational and neutral as U.N.O.

The costumes we wore for these performances were made by local volunteers. We went to the houses of several spinster-ladies with sweet, sad faces, to be measured and fitted. They were devoted to missionary work but uncertain needlewomen. They induced in us a kind of vague excitement as their fingers travelled around our limbs. They had only the sketchiest ideas about the geographical context of the clothes they were designing for us. They were at their safest when we had been cast as Amazonian Stone Age Men or Equatorial pygmies wearing only the type of minimal clout prescribed by the Defence of the Realm Act. On at least one occasion I walked on to the stage in the part of a Chinese Mandarin determined to keep Confucius and Calvin frigidly apart, and dressed exactly in the uniform of a short Rhondda Valley bus conductor. This got a clap from a reactionary fringe of people in the back row, who thought that missionary work was long overdue among transport workers.

Our Sunday school teacher was a sad, many-faced man to whom in the long hard run we owed a great deal. His name was Bryn. He was a harassed primary school teacher and a frustrated musician. He had had several love affairs pulled out from under him by handsome interlopers. He, with his music, would bring the girls to a state of maximum pliancy, and the actual manipulation would be done by the sexual Vikings of the village, who were always to be found prowling at the mouth of every accessible fjord.

His nerves had been further bruised by the fact that his father had been responsible for some innocent bit of mismanagement of the Boot Fund or some such welfare enterprise. The money involved could not have been more than a few shillings, for the local urge to provide boots for the needy was not dynamic, but local gossip had raised Bryn's father to the status of Ivar Kruger.

Even as a Sunday school teacher his luck was not in. At a time when, emotionally, he was losing every battle he fought, he found himself confronted by a covey of fierce young dialecticians still in short trousers but provided with a nightly round of Voltairian shot by the sages in the Institute, and we had Bryn squarely in our sights.

At the time of his greatest philosophic crisis with us, he was in love with one of the chapel organists, a brisk and lovely blonde and a skilled hand with the more pounding type of voluntary. She took a low view of us and told Bryn that if he had any sense he would drop us over the gallery of the vestry, or ship us to the Orinoco to play out our last missionary sketch the hard way.

To impress her he promised us all a half-crown each if we learned in Welsh the entire Sermon on the Mount. This was big money and for a week we burned our brain-linings to become word perfect. We turned up the next Sunday bursting with greed and the urge to declaim. We found Bryn silent and beyond the reach of our voices. We took turns at giving out in our loud alto voices the golden words about the meek and the pure in heart. But he was not on our earth. The organist had run away a day before with a travelling china-salesman, who had had affairs with half the responsive women in the valley, and paid them with vases of a gaudy and plateresque kind.

His answer to us was music. He had, for that period, a magnificent collection of gramophone records, all operatic. During the sessions of the Band of Hope he played to us the voices of Caruso, Chaliapin, Melba, Destinn. The effect of hearing things like the Death of Boris, Tamagno as Otello, Tito Ruffo as Carlo Gerard, is as fresh with me now as it was then. It opened an experience whose echoes are still knocking about in every corner of my life. We relaxed and smiled in a cloud of beauty, and when we looked at Bryn, would wish that the shadow of autocratic dogma had never fallen between us.

Bryn was also a chronic producer of Biblical cantatas, some of which, I think, he wrote himself. He was obsessed in the matter of themes with that part of the Old Testament which deals with the wild, violent characters like Jezebel, Samson, Elijah, the clash of Israelite and Philistine, the struggle for dominance in the minds of the terrified desert dwellers of Yaweh and Baal.

The chorus would be divided equally, at first, between Israelites and Philistines. The assistant choir-master was a colliery official whom we found to be baleful. He was harsh in his personal idiom and unbelievably conservative in his social thinking. He was for the Israelites through thick and thin, and he saw to it that his personal favourites were prominent in that faction of the choir. He thrust me and my companions to the back row of the Philistines. But as the weeks went by and his baton took on the function of scorpion and knout, a drift in our direction set in, and by the eve of the performance the great majority were on our side of the stage, rooting for Baal at the top of our voices and giving our principal baritone, who was playing Elijah, such a case of the shakes he switched at the last moment to another vestry group which was staging *Floradora*.

A few weeks ago I saw the old chapel again. I stood at a certain distance away, as if afraid that the vibrant delight and ironies of the past might still have the power to touch, enchant and hurt me. Faces and voices came out of the place. The deacon thundering into the darkness behind the chapel, where pairs and even trios of lovers were seeking expression against the back wall of the chapel. 'No undue violence of movement among you rodneys. There is subsidence!'

And subsidence there certainly was. The only serious interruption in the flow of coin towards the missionary effort was when one of the chapel walls threatened to fall inwards upon the congregation. If the cadence was outwards, a few rough bastions of wood and a warning to the public to watch out and jump clear were considered enough. The place must have had a frailer fabric than any twelfth-century chapel, the one place of faith in whose rafters the death-watch beetle took one look and refused to watch.

The genial tenor, Watkins, was known from some act of cunning in youth as Will False. Each Quarterly Meeting he would sing the same song, 'Nirvanah', the lyric of which was clear in its praise and encouragement of Buddhism. If the words of the song had been properly understood, Watkins would either have been regarded as carrying on in his traditional line of deviousness or asked never to sing again. As Watkins made his way down the aisle to sing he had his coat pulled by a member of the congregation called Maldwyn Morgan. This Morgan was a perverse Marxist who remained a member of the chapel only to worry Moscow. He was sometimes known, as a tribute to his powers as a Left-wing Marxist, as Maldwyn the Negation of the Negation. Watkins stopped to hear what Morgan had to say.

'What song have you got for us this time, Watkins?' He asked the question in a rough, truculent way because Morgan, at any time, would have preferred a speech to a vocal solo. Besides, there were certain

piercing effects that Watkins managed in 'Nirvanah' which bent
Morgan's headbones.

'"Nirvanah", Mr Morgan. I'm going to sing that tested favourite,
"Nirvanah".'

'The one that gives a boost to Buddha?'

'That's the one.'

'Watkins,' said Morgan, after a pause that made the congregation
think that Morgan had now crowned his career of political mischief by
hypnotising Watkins and bringing the quarterly meeting to a halt.
'Watkins, you are little better than an Oriental deviationist.'

Harry, the cockle-man, who roamed the valleys with a cart, selling
cockles, scandalising women with his method of freshening his wares.
He was not by any means a regular communicant, but after some wild
and suicidal bender, getting his horse as drunk as he was, and sleeping on
his cockles when he needed an interval of rest from joy, he would come
into the chapel porch and peer in at the service through one of the
windows. Not any part of the window, but one particular pane of deep
blue glass, to see through which he had to stand on tip-toe. This view
seemed to give him some ease and, after staring for five minutes into his
little indigo universe, he would totter out as normal as he ever would be.
There is a legend that Harry was once returning home with his horse and
cart from a sales trip to Abertillery. He had spent a few days in that town
and drawn the attention of the police on himself for some outstanding
bits of coarse behaviour. Playing it safe he had spent one whole evening,
not in the pub, but a cinema. He had seen *Ben Hur*, the silent version
with Ramon Navarro. The chariot race had enthralled him.

The next morning he got drunk and mounted his cart and picked up
his reins, but this time with a difference. He was in Rome and in his head
was no thought of cockles. He whipped the horse and yelled at it and left
the town at a good canter, the horse wondering why Harry should now
be wanting to choke it after so many years of friendship, the people of
Abertillery wondering, after a quick leap into the nearest doorway, if
this might be a last refugee from Boadicea's last campaign. Down the
valley road went Harry, his pace increasing by the minute. He was, by
now, every inch the charioteer, his face imperious, his body bent right
back to lessen its weight on the cart. The only reason the horse did not
complain was that it had taken a look at Harry's stance and was con-
vinced that Harry would fall out before the nonsense went any further.
He did not. They thundered towards Crumlin. Crumlin has the highest

viaduct in Wales. Harry looked up at it, stared appraisingly at his horse, laughed demoniacally and shouted, 'Now under this one, you b——.'

A sporadic sectary, Harry, but he spoke to us from a wasteland that we wanted, in oblique ways, to know, and colonise.

Mr Paul, the nearest we ever came to a political boss. Once he stood in for Bryn as our Sunday school teacher, but his disenchantment and ours came together to form a glacial whole and off he went, shivering and vowing to stick to politics where the average pair of eyes had grown dim and unexpecting.

Mr Paul had been a councillor for many years. For the larger part of his administrative course he worked with such zeal and integrity he exhausted his seam of service, and gave out hollow sounds when touched. As poverty grew there was talk of small financial deals arranged to fix the allocation of this job or that. The word nepotism was used but required the use of a footnote so often it was dropped. One councillor was offered a chicken in exchange for his vote in the appointment to a certain headmastership, and was so outraged he carried this fowl about from meeting to meeting, holding it up as a measure of the turpitude that was now encamped in local affairs. His revelations fell on soil frozen with indifference. The only reaction was a will to save on the part of candidates for jobs who were short of a chicken, or a demand from audiences, after two or three weeks, that the councillor should either shut up or get a fresh bird.

We watched this development with real interest. The molten stream of idealism that had flowed through our collective head had been so destructively hot, the coming of a little cool corruption struck a note of astonishing novelty. Mr Paul's shoulders grew heavy, and his head sank down as if afraid to meet any eye that looked likely to send an infra-red challenge to the strange things that were stirring and breeding in the cellars of his conscience. During the singing of hymns his lips did not stir, as if his mind could not stand even the lightest load of pure lyricism. At public meetings he could trot out his immemorial jests as glibly as ever.

'So the doctor said, "Mrs Evans, give Evans this pill." "Will it cure him of what he's got, doctor?" "I don't know. But it'll give him hiccups and I'm a dab hand with hiccups."

'And that, brothers, is an exact portrait of the way capitalism goes about the job of curing its current wasting sickness. So the doctor said, "Mrs Bevan, your husband is undernourished to a point where he and the fruit fly are running neck and neck. He must be given food that will

The Elder

give him a quick lift. I suggest champagne and oysters." Now this man was a long-range pauper, a full-stop of dereliction even for these parts. So his wife did the best she could. Cockles and pop.

'My enemies paint me as a wicked man. They say that I'm about with women and so on. Of course I am. I get my concubines sent up from Cardiff by the crate. Five bob back on the empties.'

When Mr Paul was in the last dark bloom of cynicism, a young Independent councillor, who for years had been breaking his reformist teeth on the crusted shell of the ruling caucus, decided to retire in disgust. He decided also at the last meeting he attended to get off his chest a definitive judgment on Mr Paul.

'Mr Paul,' he said, 'do you know what you are?'

Mr Paul, wise, cold and hard as the Eiger, sat quite still and waited to be told.

'Mr Paul,' said the Lancelot of the lower gulch, 'you are an incorrigible lecher, a dedicated peculator and an unregenerate renegade.'

Mr Paul looked up and asked, 'Is that a sarcastic taunt?'

I walked closer to the chapel. I waited or hoped to savour more fully the flavour of its mouldering emptiness. It was not empty. It was not mouldering. It was full of children's voices and whirring metallic sounds. It had become a skating rink.

10 Cardiff and her Smaller Sisters

THE Normans came in from the sea and coal came down from the hills. The coal made even more money than the Normans, and a gaggle of cottages around a huge castle became a city which has at last managed to get itself recognised as the capital of Wales.

Its claims to pre-eminence are challenged by townships whose title deeds to being the capital are often inscrutable. One will assert that John Elias preached his longest sermon there, and wants some compensation even though it is a hundred and thirty years late. Another will claim to have staged the only Eisteddfod in which the winning tenor, by vocal force alone, kept the canvas wholly clear of the marquee poles. In a third one, one of Wales's early harassed princes, who emerge from history books as having been almost continuously on the run, paused and uttered a prophecy of ruin before going on to the next leg of his unhappy marathon. Our annals are full of doom-laden utterances, and they have kept up a pretty steady level of accuracy.

But Cardiff, to all but a few Welshmen, is the city. The whole sweep of the south-east Glamorgan landscape around it has a magic pattern. Northward from Cardiff, like the fingers of a bruised hand, shoot the great valleys that would have produced, given a little more attention and a little less rain, a culture of brilliant vitality. One half of Cardiff is the life that streams into it from the northern hills. For millions of children from the Rhondda Cardiff has been the nerve-end of all delight, the glare at the end of the tunnel, their first contact with a well-lit urbanity, the first visible evidence of wealth and ease.

For one who lives in Cardiff but who once made his first journey there down the railway that rushes through Porth and Pontypridd, the walk along Queen Street towards the castle can never be undertaken without a tremor of expectation. The sensation is helped by the fact that Cardiff is a city of the most inexplicable draughts. Around the General Station in particular, a family of winds has got itself stuck and there has been no one to show them the way out. They reproduce in their tempo and sound the tumultuous anxieties of the travellers inside the station.

It is quite a place, that main terminal in Cardiff. South Wales has been one of the classic lands of emigration. If a South Walian wants to look at his motherland he has to keep turning, for his brothers are every-where. And it is on the platforms of Cardiff General that the shattered heart reassembles. One could not count the number of times one has seen two or more Welshmen come out of their train, and as they hurry on to the next stage of their journey, one hears them shout, 'See you in Cardiff the day of the match. In the Park, the Queen's, the Grand, the Royal.' Or whatever bar or cinema front takes their fancy.

Cardiff is the settled Zion of the Welsh Israelites. A face you may have glimpsed in Maerdy, Ammanford, Treharris, Blaencwm, and thought never on this earth to see again, be sure that one winter's after-noon it will come again into view in the swift river of people that flows down Quay Street towards the gates of the Arms Park.

The Arms Park is the great shrine. The memories of the great games that have been played there have been worn as smooth as pebbles by every talking group in the taverns and clubs of the region. They have become, for many, a sort of ritual incantation which has come close to ousting the theological and political jousts of yesteryear. Men who were not born at the time will come to blows over who scored the try that beat the All Blacks in 1905. The only person in the nook who was really there says nothing. After thirty years of recounting the epic he shut up for good in 1935.

If you have that over-forty feeling and are quietly dusting your policies, come and stand in a capacity crowd at the Arms Park when they sing one of the great hymns. The sadder the hymns the better, because that allows the boys to dig deep for their harmonies. It is typical of us that if the hospitality is lavish, we are often married and buried to the rhythm of the same superb graveside chants. At the Arms Park it is like being caught up in some mighty natural force; it gives you a taste of what it must have been like to be caught up in the fierce, hypnotic frenzies of tribalism.

Even notoriously discourteous spectators, whose banter has peeled the paint off the old stand, have been so overwhelmed by this experience they have gone through the entire match glassy-eyed and opening their

136

mouths only to advise the referee to wear longer knicks when the colder weather comes. But our choral tradition is crumbling somewhat. The vast anthems of yearning melancholy are often displaced by flimsier tunes, and the folk on the two-bob bank, being chilled, sing to a brisker measure than the cosier choristers in the stands, and the first group can often be well into the third verse when the rearguard is still edging its way out of the overture. This, in so vocally conscious an area, is going to cause some heavy neuroses. But even now, on form, the lads can blow a hole in heaven and reduce a complete military band to the status of a solitary fifer on an upland.

The speaking voices of this city fascinate. The immigrant half, the visitors from the hills, speak with a singing intonation, as if every sentence is half-way into oratorio, the vowels as broad as their shoulders. The Cardiff speech, a compound of the native dialect and a brand of High Bristolian, gives an impression of a worldly hardness. They speak of 'Cairdiff', 'Cathays Pairk', and for a long time it is not amiable to the ear. There is an edge of implied superiority in it to the rather innocent and guileless openness of the valley-speech. As you move towards the docks, an area still on the dark and ghetto-like side, you hear the high, soft speech of a hundred tongues from Africa and the East, or perhaps from the lips of a child born into the docks, an enchanting mixture of Somerset, Madagascar and Pontllanfraith.

The docks do not live as abundantly as they did. There is always a little blood on the moon in the economic life of this zone. The hills, if you count out some pretty active patches of subsidence in the valleys, are fairly steady, but industrial trends have been on the jumpy side. The stress on coal, as we see it now, was a deadly, paralysing truss. The truss is broken but cramps linger. The rise of Cardiff as a port is one of the great dramatic tales of British commercial history. Between 1890 and 1920 so much coal left these wharves, we marvel that the world is ever cold or that we have anything left to stand on.

The dynasty of Cardiff tycoons, Lord Glanely and the rest, hard and resolute as the crews they sent out to the oceans, set their mark upon the city. Cory Hall commemorates one of the greatest coalowners. The lovely Temple of Peace stands witness to the zeal of Lord Davies of Llandinam, who put his fortune to work in the cause of international unity and peace. It was a relatively simple world they lived in. A hustling commerce had coal as practically the single currency. The British merchant marine was supreme.

We know what happened to coal. Markets shrank as conflict in the

City Hall Clock

coalfield grew. We, who knew the coal valleys as children during the twenties, saw so many long stoppages of work we almost regarded life as a lunatic escapade in which normality just dropped flat on its face every whipstitch. 'If you are good you can have an idle pit for Christmas,' was one of the merrier proverbs of the time. There were local pigeons that tried to shed their homing instinct before each big race. The mansions of Cardiff's docksmen edged into a sad dusk as flats and offices. History will dismiss the whole thing as a growing-pain. Today, the Cardiff docks, like the rest of South Wales, are finding their way to a more varied and reliable activity.

In the city's centre is a patch of noble amenity in marble and granite. Wealth did not come too long before civic pride here, and there is an Athenian grace about the group of buildings, the County and City Halls, the Museum, the Law Courts, that extend the castle's dignity on the city's northern side. Among the buildings are bits of memorial statuary. To the artist they bring no comfort, and to the social historian they are odd. The men remembered were, without doubt, wise, brave or rich, but a bronze frock coat, considered as deathless art, does not even get started.

South Walians are proud of this city centre. The museum, in itself and in the things it encloses, is a place of miraculous beauties. South Walians generally point to this parkland of gracious architecture with a somewhat angry pride. Angry because their valleys are a syllabus of every error that can make human dwellings of a repellent unworthiness. Long streets laid out like grey bruises on the soaked and puzzled hills; places of public assembly apparently designed by sinister misanthropes to keep the public dispersed. Let the valley dweller, or for that matter a resident of Bute Street or Grangetown, step forth from Kingsway and head towards the University College buildings, and he will have intimations of a lush and laundered future.

The modern history of Cardiff's castle has a fair number of ironical turns. These Welsh castles never fail to give the historical fancy a kick. Most of them are a low, defensive mutter in an alien, hating land. Time and ruin have brought them a pathos of peace. But the steady residence of the Butes in this pile has given it a lived-in, manorial touch. It now belongs to the Cardiff Corporation.

The Third Estate crowds in to stroll and glance at a shilling a head, bemused at being on the domestic hearth of the power against which they have been waging a stubborn rearguard action for the last nine hundred years. A ghastly blockage, castles.

Part of the castle is now a College of Music and Drama. The visitor can listen simultaneously to the wailing ghost of Robert of Normandy, who spent twenty years here in a type of deep well, and the uncertain sounds of art in its rough stage.

The rebuilt section of the castle, through which tourists are conducted in gasping groups (astonishment and stairs activate the gasps), is a nineteenth-century flourish of triumphant wealth. The Chaucer room, a bed-chamber with a conical ceiling made up of illustrations in coloured glass of Chaucer's tales, in which some privileged insomniac might well have dropped off while counting Canterbury lambs. There is a room designed to reproduce the reclining chamber of a harem which always causes a thoughtful pursing of lips among the more dour puritans from the hills.

There is a table with a hole in the middle through which a vine grew, allowing the resident Marquis to pluck his fruit fresh from the bough while broaching his meat. This has brought many a cry of envy from the visitors, as if a meal eaten without a canopy of verdure is a fraud. The library, when stocked, was a thing of glowing, gold-leaved joy, but the books have gone and the chamber, despite its magnificent woods, is nerveless and inert. There is a decorative motif of bronze monkeys in the centre of which precious stones once glittered, but the stones have been taken away and the monkeys just look bereft and sardonic about the whole business.

Flanking the castle and also available now to the ratepayers is a stretch of the most enchanting parkland which goes clear up to Llandaff, a curious wedge of medieval quietness stuck between the stridencies of Cardiff and the mining belt. The park has become a great lung of liberty for the young. On a Saturday morning a dozen school football teams can do their best in a setting of woodland to which autumn brings a beauty that would move a mule to tears. The castle peeps over the trees, a stronger heart than ever before for a fine, strong city. It is good when the past accepts and gives such a friendly handshake to the present.

There are other places that lay claim to primacy, some in tones of the most sincere eloquence, others in terms of the most desperate irony. Take Bedlinog.

*   *   *

It was a very high noon when I landed in Bedlinog. The look of the place surprised me. It did not have the defiant ugliness of most mining villages. It has something else, though. A tip that burns, poisons, depresses and annoys each and every villager.

I looked around. There was a nice balance of pubs and chapels. There was no sign of the thing I had come to look for.

A massive man, who looked like Hemingway, was sitting on a bench in a posture of magisterial despair. I took him to be a victim of the smell. 'Where is it?' I asked.

'Where's what?' He sounded as if he had gone beyond wanting to locate anything.

'The tip that burns and smells. The tip they are spraying with scent to sweeten it.' This was the current plum of Welsh absurdity I had come to track down.

The old man jerked his head upwards. 'You'll find it,' he said.

I started to climb. Bedlinog is virtually a wall. After ninety minutes' trudging I was a puffing hoop. I was checking on strokes in my first-aid manual when it struck me. The Smell. It was as if the world had suddenly grown old. At the very first whiff of it gaiety dropped dead. I walked down a side-street and there it was. A few acres of fuming blackness.

On the further sides were the poles from which the scent can be sprinkled. At the tip's foot was the little hut from which this miracle is engineered. An object with a silver glint was fixed to one of the poles. This was the wind-indicator, which tells when the vapours are being blown townward, and announces to Bedlinog that it has qualified for its shower of deodorant. Bedlinog's flavour is described thus by the manufacturer's chemist: 'If you sat under a pine tree sucking a lemon you would have something of the idea.'

South Wales is full of things that people forgot to sweep up. And the tips in the Merthyr-Bedlinog area have always had a name for militant malodour. It is said that during the influenza epidemics between the wars the degree of immunity in this zone was abnormally high. The germs just couldn't even break even.

The collieries, of which the sixty-year-old tip is the product, yielded splendid coal. Their output in the 1914–18 war went to the Navy. The Navy wanted only the best, the purest fuel. That meant that coal was poured into the tip as sub-standard which today would be offered to the public without a blush as good enough.

Indeed, part of this very tip which is now burning like a sub-station of the cremation centres on the Ganges, is currently being torn apart by a company which specialises in giving old tips a going-over for saleable coal and the raw material for such articles as breeze-blocks.

When the scandal began, the emission of evil fumes was such that trees withered, nostrils shrank and a threepenny rate was mooted for the provision of a vast, municipal iron lung for the frailer voters.

Now comes the gesture of the cherry atop the whole black trifle. Scenting or deodorising one's follies could well catch on.

'We have a plague coming up. How would you like it? Lilac?'

'There's a war cooking. Will lavender do?'

We see the nice, humanitarian point of the scent sprays. But, with the moon just a whistle-stop away, I think we could land there with a bit more confidence if, first, we could do something about the tip in Bedlinog.

* * *

In all the valleys of the South Welsh mountains we find the power and turbulence of men, dedicated to making their world stronger, more reliable and dirtier. Steel-making has drifted down towards the coast, to Newport, to Port Talbot and Cardiff. Ebbw Vale alone remains among the hills from which the early ironmasters sheared the trees for fuel.

There is nothing in Ebbw Vale but steel. It is the place associated with Aneurin Bevan, orator, dreamer, wit. He took the image of this place out of the valleys in which he was born and presented it, its imperfections, its struggles, its humour, as a challenge to those parts of Britain that have never been scarred by poverty or the monstrous toll that heavy industry exacts from beauty.

When we look at these people, these streets, strung precariously around that central dark fist of steel-making, you will catch the echoes of that half-impish, half-angry irony that ran through the thought and the speeches of Bevan.

The sheer problem of moving about on such slopes is considerable. Thirty years of swift movement up and down these streets develops leg muscles of a size that disqualifies one for the ballet, and did much to bankrupt half our tailors, who switched over to making pants for rhinos. There was no excitement to match that of the valley children pelting down these tilting streets on winter nights, down into the lighted town. But the journey up for the not so young could be a torment, and boys like the young Aneurin Bevan must have earned more than one odd copper pushing some decrepit citizen up to one of the top terraces. There was a lot to be said, we thought as babies, for taking out a permanent ticket in the pram.

From the moment man began to fiddle with his first furnace he was, like the sparks he created, on his way upwards. To re-create the heat of the sun from which he sprang, that was the task. He could never go back to coolness and calmness after that. When he learned to blow the impurities out of iron bubbling away at infernal temperatures, he had taken Nature firmly by the hand and the time was ripe for the vast, pounding hammers that were to beat out the tools and weapons of the modern age.

To the children of South Wales, who grew up familiar with the sights of open furnaces making the night sky crimson, such works as these were the eyes of the world. Over the last century the men who make steel have sweated enough to put out all the fires on earth. To live in a half-molten, incandescent world drains the body of moisture. And man, being a watery animal, needs to have it put back. In the old days the men were allowed to restore the balance with buckets of beer, but this practice ceased when it was found that workers with the larger type of thirst and the broader type of bucket, took too flippant a view of the industry after the refreshment break.

After a man has handled molten metal, treating it as casually as a boy would a glass of pop, life must be a bit of a let-down. I seem to see in the faces of steel-workers, when they are relaxing at the day's end, a grave melancholy as if they had seen it all, as indeed they have.

Ebbw Vale stands at the head of the valley. It is a confined place. To the south you will pass through towns that sprang out of the writhing need for coal and steel, towns like Aberbeeg and Cwm, where the streets are like a petrified meringue, twirled out of plumb by the twists and turns of the hillsides.

But to the north there is an astonishing other world. Down from the moorland come the wild ponies, creatures that roam the streets of Ebbw Vale in a kind of democratic brotherhood with the citizens. And sheep-dogs foxed by living in a world half pastoral, half industrial, trapped by their neuroses into not knowing exactly what they are supposed to be rounding up.

It was here, over the moorland, that Aneurin Bevan often walked. The moorland and the pub at the end of the outward stroll restored him after the tight, oppressive rounds of political disturbance, and all the problems of fuel, movement and direction could, for a moment or two, be forgotten. This was the other side of his life, and one which explains his moods, the contradictions that scurried across his life like clouds across a sky. For the men of the valleys live in two worlds. They know, on the one hand, the noise, the disfigurements, the failures of industrial man, and just up the hillside over the ridge, a pastoral calm that has never seriously been breached.

Men like Bevan know there is no going back to the simplicity, the reliable goodness of fern-covered plateaux, ploughed fields, the companionship of animals, whom not even a politician needs to distrust. For it is not likely that the horse will be given the vote for some time yet. All the same, when a man has a paradise of trees and fields half an hour's walking distance from his own street, he is going to find it harder to accept that street if it is sunk too far below the level of dignity and delight he expects for his neighbours and himself. Once you have heard the lark, known the swish of feet through hill-top grass and smelt the earth made ready for the seed, you are never again going to be fully happy about the cities and the towns that man carries like a crippling weight upon his back.

Ebbw Vale first came into my orbit about twelve years ago when a novel of mine appeared with a title that did little to cheer up South Wales, *All Things Betray Thee.* The story told of a wandering harpist of the 1830's who comes southward to find a friend, who has become involved in one of the conflicts that seared the history of the early iron industry in what we now call the Western valleys.

The book opens with the harpist striding over the last ridge that divides him from the region where the furnaces alternately darkened and reddened the sky.

It was not until several years later that I understood fully what the physical impact of that experience would have been.

I had been invited, in the days when I was functioning as a bijou sage, to take part in a Brains Trust to be held at the Social and Recreational club of the Richard Thomas & Baldwin steelworks at Ebbw Vale. It was a winter's night of the most fierce brand, and my driver had never before ventured a yard along the road from Newport to Ebbw Vale, a road that oscillates as sharply and unpredictably as the graph of a lie-detector. He lost the way disastrously at Aberbeeg and Cwm. After the second diversion he asked me if I really believed in brains trusts. If not we could double back to Newport and nip up to a village near Usk, where he knew a man who sold poached salmon.

But we pushed on and that was my first experience of Ebbw Vale. Its street lamps shot dramatically up the hillsides, and the steel-works provided the town with its central diamond of brilliant light. My driver made one or two more mistakes, including a short tour of the steel-works. He was convinced that the Social Club of a steel plant would be conducted within sight of the furnace's glare.

When I got to the Brains Trust it was booming and I was not even being missed. At the session's end the audience, a large group of young people all living in Ebbw Vale, answered questions put to them by the panel. I have rarely heard any young people more intelligent, more articulate, more human. I was to find on later visits that there is a crackling mental vitality about the whole place. In South Wales there are few towns where books, the theatre and politics have such bright and powerful partisans.

The night of the Brains Trust I spent in the Red Lion at Llangynidr on the Breconshire side of Ebbw Vale. It is an ancient inn in an enchanting village, geographically quite near the steel town, but in quality and tradition a thousand miles apart. Legend says that the Red Lion was built as a country house for Anne Boleyn during one of Henry VIII's frequent fits of pique.

The following morning I woke early. The sun was strong and smiling as if trying to apologise for all the trouble I had had the night before at Aberbeeg and Cwm. I walked out into the garden. Facing me was the most gigantic mastiff I had ever seen. First I thought it might have been the ghost of Anne Boleyn's horse. My next thought was to show the hound some astonishing footwork and bolt the door.

After breakfast I decided to do the journey back to Ebbw Vale on foot, a strange choice for a man who practically invented the chair. It was probably the combined shock of seeing the sun and feeling like a dish of dog food.

It was a remarkable journey. I can think of no other that underscores so dramatically the two faces of South Wales, the man-made face of mighty industries and brutally inadequate townships, and the face of moorland, wood and field that has changed little except in rateable value since time began.

*   *   *

The mind is full of remembered places where one thought one located the central nerve of Wales. There is the village of Llandarrog, in Carmarthenshire, where the lines of the church and the surrounding trees sing and woo like Romeo and Juliet. It has an inn with such a wealth of ancient and mellow wood-work, black oak, that even if woodworm struck, it would be prepared to accept a quiet drink and do no damage. The tone of old, dark wood is thematic, inescapable. As you sip the ale you think of sap and see the first traces of medullary rings in your companions.

Beyond Llandarrog westward, a great swish of rising and falling road brings you to Carmarthen town, where the opening hours on market days, and the secretiveness of the farmers coming in to trade from the valley of the Cothi, create the impression of a subtle haze. Perversely Carmarthen voted against the opening of pubs on a Sunday. They possibly voted this way to show their shock at discovering that the pubs had ever closed.

The town contains one of the country's quainter ancient monuments, Merlin's Oak. It is a ravaged stump. When it falls, Wales, the legend says, will be in trouble. Thinking that things were tough enough already the citizens buttressed the tree in a coat of cement. There is talk now that a new road scheme might put paid to this timeless landmark. Either we should explain to the Minister of Transport that Wales can ill afford to lose a good-luck emblem of this sort, or we should ring up Merlin for more cement.

A less inscrutable erection is the equestrian statue of General Picton, who died at Waterloo. Which was a silly thing to do when he could have got off his horse and settled for a life of deep, uproarious tap-room talk in this sweet and subtle town.

I have tender feelings for Cardigan Town with its sister township, St Dogmaels, just over the estuary. The circumstances of my first seeing the mouth of the Teifi endear both places to me.

It was the beginning of the war. I was living in Manchester and I would have hated it even if the Germans had not currently been bombing the place. When I had the chance of a teaching job in Cardigan I jumped, partly at the job, partly to dodge a bomb.

I paused at Neath on my way west. The Germans seemed to be following me about, for they dropped bombs there too. One of these blew me out of my braces which retained their normal working position, rigid with shock.

I was taken to Cardigan on a lorry belonging to a friend of mine. He was a man who never took his eyes off the road or his tongue off the topic he happened to be pursuing. The door on my side of the lorry had a defective lock. As we neared Carmarthen my friend was throwing the light on the situation in France, at that moment unusually murky. He swung the lorry around Carmarthen bridge, the door sprang open and I went rolling like a hoop towards the Towy. My friend was on the further side of Carmarthen and still explaining France before he noticed that I had left the cab.

The mishap left me with a cricked back and a dramatic stoop. During my few days in Cardigan I was treated as a victim of the bombings and feted as a hero. And that is how I first landed on the enchanting Bay of Cardigan.

In St Dogmael's there are the shadowed fishermen's pubs full of dark tales of deadly battles with the water-bailiffs, illicit baits and midnight massacres of salmon. After listening to these sagas of treachery and guile, I would say that the salmon, a fish about which an undue fuss has always been made, would be well advised to stay put in the Gulf Stream.

*   *   *

The Vale of Glamorgan has always been a kind of heartland to me. As children we stood on the Trebanog ridge and surveyed the great expanse of coloured fields and tranquil villages merging into the sea. It was all so different from the narrow, enclosed life we knew in the valleys.

Later on, when our limbs could stand it, we ventured forth on walking tours down to the coast. The expedition would usually be disastrous. The family would pack enough food for us to justify them in the hope that they had seen the back of us for a week. We would take the road bent almost double beneath the fodder and a type of tent that went out of date in the Boer War. By the time we reached Pendoylan we had contracted every type of blister known and a few that were original.

And by the time we reached the little cove to which we might be

149

Vale of Glamorgan farmhouse

heading, Monknash or Marcross, we would simply sit down, belt the
week's ration at a sitting, make a few suicidal manœuvres with the tent-
pole, then wrap the canvas around us and sleep until the lighthouse
keeper at Nash Point threatened to treat us as flotsam and cast us off if
we didn't bestir ourselves.

On the northern rim of the Vale of Glamorgan is Llantrisant, built as
a fortress town to keep a stony, commanding eye on the coastal plain. If
Glamorgan needed a capital this could be it. From the beginning of time
it has been a centre of military turbulence. From here the embattled hill-
folk probably told the trampling Normans to stay home and stop being a
nuisance. The slopes are sharp and punishing. Ancient warriors attacking
this citadel never had enough breath left to explain where they had come
from. This confused historians.

It is an enclosed, mysterious place, still living a life very much of its
own, quite distinct from the mining valleys and the farmlands to the
south. Once there were so many pubs here the church had a cork spire.
Here in the memory of men still living, the miners of the Rhondda came

150

Llantrisant

to roister. They arrived by trap and left by float. Time is ripe and mellow here. The old men relish and sip it as if it were ale. A cautious place. The name suggests that. Llantrisant, the church with the three saints. Most churches make do with one but here the sinners had a triple indemnity.

They still call the men of Llantrisant the Black Prince's men. On the edge of the village is the Black Prince's Tower, the mouldering finger of what was once a pretty mighty fist. Now the only living things among these gnawed walls are beehives and the man who keeps them. The bees are the only inheritors, the only echo of the fury that once buzzed here. The whole place is a honeycomb of time. Ivy and silence. And it is nice to think of bees taking over from the pomp and terror that once encamped there.

The news of the day laps the residue of centuries. Is the Black Prince a ghostly presence or the latest thing to take off from Cape Canaveral? Llantrisant now is rarely in the news. Some stubborn rearguard action by the citizens to safeguard their common land against housing or opencast mining, and little more.

The last great scandalous excitement here was the case of Dr William Price, pioneer of cremation in a zone dedicated to fuel problems. When he erected his first pyre he was nearly lynched by the townsfolk who insisted that he should play it cool. He was a rabid eccentric who kept whippets of the area on edge by wearing a rabbit-skin hat with the tail hanging down the back.

In a pub called The Star, at Wick, down on the coast near Llantwit Major, is an illustrated broadsheet of Price's own cremation. We see a picture of Price dressed in the costume he wore as the high priest of the newly revived cult of Druidism, which did little to make the Welsh problem any more penetrable. Also in the picture is Price's son, to whom he gave the name, acceptable in Spain but shocking in Wales, Jesus.

My father claimed to have seen Price. He used to come over to the Rhondda from Llantrisant, in his fur hat and riding a horse. Once, in Trebanog, he was told of a young woman who was gravely ill and quite prepared, in her supreme misery, to die. Dr Price looked at her and simply shook his head when asked by the neighbours to proclaim the sickness, and declare its cure.

Then he said, 'Has anyone here got a pair of very young kittens?' The kittens were brought. 'Put one under each of her arms and tell her to keep them there for twenty-four hours.'

He got back on his horse.

'Will that cure her?' someone asked.

Ebbw Vale

'I don't know,' said Price. 'But life is warmth and kittens give out great heat. Besides, if she can keep two kittens under her arms for twenty-four hours it'll take her mind off whatever it is that's urging her to die. And that's bound to help.'

*   *   *

South Wales has few places that can be singled out and lingered over. We have not had the good fortune to have towns of deep and striking beauty like Bath or Sidmouth. Even John Betjeman, with his masterly eye for spotting odd bits of neglected loveliness, would find it hard to view an average mining village with anything but a puzzled frown. We may not have deliberately gone after beauty with a hatchet, but in the majority of our townships beauty has managed to get itself scalped.

What we do have is drama. Startling studies in contrast and change. This is perfectly illustrated in a swift trip through mid-Glamorgan, the territory between Pontypridd and Merthyr, land of tough men, lovely women, tall mountains, deep coal-seams and a record collection of perpendicular streets.

Pontypridd is the Damascus of Glamorgan. Like Aberdare it is a mining town grafted on to an ancient market centre. When I went back there the flood of shoppers and pleasure-seekers was still swilling down from the adjoining valleys. The salesmen at the market booths were as loud and fascinating as ever. I saw the pitch where once, long ago, a crystal-ball reader called 'The New Merlin' had a sign outside his tent which ran, 'The Future Told, cautiously'. It was a period when that sort of statement made sense.

I also paid my respects to the successor of the remarkable cheap-jack who, in the fastest patter since Barnum, would offer for sale anything from the Old Bridge to the police inspector's helmet. He sold me my first cigarette lighter, a contraption based on the palm-oil and bamboo model of the Orinoco Indians. Two years later I went back to him for a fresh thumb and to thank him for the first and only flame I produced from this lighter.

I strolled around the cinemas that I once haunted. There was one that started a health campaign in the middle of a biting winter; we just sat there as the manager came around with his spray, and we could feel the Flit freezing on our faces. There was another which had a fire. In the middle of the blaze a woman was spotted sitting quite jocosely in the fourpennies. She would not leave, she said, until she had seen the serial.

In the summer of 1924 we lads of Porth marched in a solid body down

154

Pontypridd Market Day

Y Wyddfa

to Pontypridd to witness the opening of the first Woolworth store in our zone. We were as impressed as if it had been the Taj Mahal. More so. In the Taj Mahal we could not have bought a cricket bat for sixpence.

*   *   *

In a community based on great industries that can be twisted out of shape in a generation, change is bound to be convulsive and erratic. Much of South Wales does less than justice to her people. Socially far too much of its life is sub-standard. But its economic prospects are so bright as to make imperative vast and rapid strides in dealing with the stupid horse-collar of nineteenth-century squalor and inadequacy that still hangs about our neck. Within the framework of such steel centres as Llanwern, Port Talbot and Ebbw Vale, the place could become a buzzing and brilliant California.

Before this happens or while this happens, we will need a virtual rebirth of grace, gaiety and charm in some of our older townships. Make a practical move to this end and you will find yourself involved in a tangle of the most complex resistances. Local Government will never have the power or money to translate its best desires. There is a case to be made out for the belief that Local Government is the best device yet for aiding the inertia of any body of national rulers who sing Blake's 'Jerusalem' just for the laughs. The soul of most conservatism is sentimentality, and sentimentality preserves the good and the bad with indiscriminate relish.

Rebels grow to love the things which first prompted their rebellion. Change is the most threatened and hunted animal in the world. Not long ago, I suggested publicly that Ebbw Vale was less than beautiful. Civic pride sprang to arms. One councillor told me, 'I wish Nye Bevan could come back and spit his venom in your face.' How can anyone not understand that the central flame of Bevan's philosophy was a wish to take our past by the scruff of its scabrous neck and shake it clean of its immemorial dirt?

But much is being done to lay the ghosts of our old failures. Newport and Port Talbot, after the most obstinate siege of public wrath, are doing something to improve the worst traffic conditions since the Romans left. Ebbw Vale has a new, large swimming pool, and plans to demolish those incredible little streets that fringe the steel-works. Aberavon Beach aims to plant a wedge of pleasure in the rather sombre coastal kingdom of strip mills and oil refineries that stretches from Margam to Llandarcy.

I like this Aberavon Beach idea, the slapping of a little joyous paint on the face of brute industry. The man in charge is Richard Burton's brother, Graham. He and his Council will have the blessing of all whose minds have ached at the hideous physical residue of the old bed-to-work and work-to-bed philosophy.

At Swansea students have undertaken a voluntary tree-planting programme on that monstrous wilderness at Landore, an industrial Hiroshima if ever there was one. We can hope that the descendants of the metal masters whose works blackened and sterilised the place will come forward and plant an expiatory sapling.

The larger maimed places will shed their shames slowly. The smaller maimed places will find life ebbing away and will vanish.

Take Pantywaun. It is a forlorn dimple in the hills a few miles from Merthyr. Like thousands of other villages in South Wales it was thrown up to meet the housing needs of the colliery. The colliery died early in the inter-war slump. There was no reason at all why people should continue to live in Pantywaun. Architecturally it is sub-Dickensian and the tiny population created tomb-like limits for local entertainments.

It was decided to speed the liquidation of the place by withdrawing public services and transferring the people to council houses near to Merthyr. The only new, spruce thing in the village is the telephone booth installed after years of agitation, and just in time for the villagers to tell their friends that they were leaving.

I went to Pantywaun just a few weeks before the final evacuation. The day was hot. We called at the village's only pub, The Royal Hotel, a place large and unbright in the manner of so many mining-valley inns. It took us a full minute to get the door open. We were welcomed by the lady of the house. She had nothing for sale.

'I told the brewers,' she said. 'Make the wound clean, I said. Don't deliver a drop more. We'll all be gone from here week after next. I don't want the boys crying into their ale remembering the days that were good and are now gone. So I told the brewers, make the wound clean.'

*   *   *

These places make up roughly my fragment of Wales. And staring at me through a haze of omission and regret are the places I have never or have too briefly seen. There are the places where one's personal vision is constantly blocked by the broad shoulders of Borrow. Places, too, where the voices and eyes struck me as so alien and remote from my native south as to clothe the remembrance of them in a puzzled silence.

11 West and Up

I DON'T belittle those wonderful piles of rock and earth, the queen mountains of the globe, the Everests and Kilimanjaros, that sit quietly just under the sun and stare down at you with those great icy eyes. I even respect those lads who load up with ropes and cleated shoes and go gasping to the peak of Everest or Kilimanjaro, flanked by Sherpas, yetis and lecture agents.

But I have a South Wales view of mountains. I want them of a size I can live on and walk on. We have them in Glamorgan. One after another, small, smooth ranges of classic line, shortish and utterly accessible, like the dark, exuberant Celts who fiddle about at their feet. Llanwonno, the Bwlch, Rhigos, Mynydd Smilog. And across the broad, serene plateau of each run paths of springy grass, fern-lined avenues of profound tranquillity. To me this is the most precious part of Wales.

Some people would regard this view as surprising or even perverse; so, for their sake, let's move westward out of Cardiff, in the southeastern corner of Wales. (We Welshmen are most at ease when heading west. Something in the east must have scalded us pretty badly in the far past.) At Culverhouse Cross the road lifts as dramatically as a beckoning hand seen in great loneliness, and through a doorway of elms we reach the Vale of Glamorgan. As a boy I thought that nothing could excel the view of the Vale's patterned fields which we had from the highest ridges of the Rhondda, to the north, but knowing now the richness of lane and village in the Vale itself I cancel that childhood notion.

Llantrisant, Llancarfan, Llanblethian, Llanbethery. I would wish no sweeter litany for my lips. (I was going to say Llitany for my Llips. The 'll' in Welsh is one of the most diabolical sounds to produce; imagine the air leaking from a tyre with a lisping sound and you have it. Llan means simply church. Wales teems with temples. Rarely has the earth known

such an explosion of pious stone. Saints have sprung up like grass in the vales of this land of incredible greens.)

My favourite among these mellow, time-stuffed morsels is Llancarfan. It was one of the great monastic settlements of the early Middle Ages. If I know my South Wales it probably broke up over some dispute about singing, maybe some wrangle with Pope Gregory about the quality of his chant. And even now you can imagine some holy scholar, in flight from worldliness, an academic feud, or a platoon of Vikings, pausing on the lip of the lovely glen and saying: 'This is it. My legs and my heart tell me this is the place. I will rest here and stay here.'

Some years ago they found the remains of a monk who had been walled up there. Whether because of some unorthodoxy or because he was too slow to get out of the way, or too polite to tell the mason to stop, is still debated in the taproom of the Fox and Hounds, particularly there because from behind his curtain of stone the monk had been staring straight at the door of the tavern a long, long time.

How best to cross South Wales? It depends on how interested you are in people. If people bother you, the way must lie across the range of the Brecon Beacons towards the hills of Cardiganshire, via Rhayader. Rhayader is a small, ancient market town, a hub of the vast green tranquillity of mid-Wales, a complex of cosy taverns in front of which stand immobile groups of wise-looking men. Their wisdom operates on short concentrated fronts and is never dented.

The Fox and Hounds at Llancarfan

The Towy above Rhandir Mwyn

In one of the older inns is a brief history of transport in that area. We learn that in 1830 it took a coach-and-four twelve hours to do the twenty-six miles from Rhayader to Devil's Bridge. Pondering the jerky deviousness of much public transport in Wales today this almost sounds like a boast.

There is a bed in Rhayader in which George Borrow slept. All the places where George Borrow slept in this part of Wales add up to a fair-sized coma. Near Aberystwyth is a pub which is actually called the George Borrow. He must have died there. I first knew Rhayader when I was nineteen. I lunched there on a perfect June afternoon on fresh crumpets and cider. My memories of that day are as fresh as those crumpets were then, and I am still using the same brand of indigestion pills.

Shooting west from Rhayader is the Elan Valley water-works, man-made but exceptionally good to look at. Wales is full of these vast reservoirs meant to keep the great midland cities of England moist.

Ogof Twm Sion Catti

There are so many of them one wonders whether the great midland cities could not be persuaded to take the rain direct. Villages have often been flooded to make possible this apotheosis of piped water. There is a nice link between the Elan Valley and the English Romantic tradition. Shelley, on one of his innumerable love-racked escapades, came to live in a village in the valley. The valley and the village are now under several fathoms of water, which is a typically English way of dealing with the Romantic tradition. Flood it.

English cities seem to need so many reservoirs in Wales, I can see the day when we Welsh will all be standing on hilltops, the stored water lapping at our feet, cursing the English and their vampirical gullets which drain away our every shower almost before it touches ground. That is why we eagerly admit as many atomic-power stations as possible. These outfits have little charm, and as a people we pass weekly resolutions urging mankind to leave Nature alone with her secrets, but these stations might persuade the Saxon hydro-maniacs to leave parts of our territory dry.

The more southerly route is a different affair but every bit as desirable. A more alive and forthcoming region you will never find. (Like an Eskimo village when the sun shines and the hunting is good, but we sing in tune as well.) The spot on the Glamorganshire coast to which I am most constantly drawn is Southerndown. On its cliff-top it has an upswinging wave of turf that can lay a kind of tranquillity on every burning nerve.

Dunraven Castle stands near by, with the sea in front of it. At one time wrecking, the luring of ships on to the rocks, was a top activity here. The inhabitants assembled with lanterns so often and so regularly on the cliffs that ships came to rely on them, and they were taken over eventually by the authorities as being cheaper than a lighthouse.

The stretch of country between Margam Mountain and Porthcawl is of a brooding loveliness. Kenfig Pool is there in the middle of the dunes. This pool was popularly claimed to be fabulously deep and on its bed an ancient city sunk for some wickedness or sin of pride. The legend made us happy. Some of us liked it because wickedness has not done so well in the zone since the big religious revivals. The people of Kenfig liked it because being sunk out of sight was one trouble that hadn't happened to them yet.

But during the war an engineer came to live in Kenfig. He was a disputatious and sardonic man. One night, to rile his companions, he rowed out to the middle of the pool and started probing. He found the

Harlech Castle

maximum depth of the pool to be about eleven feet. He left Kenfig just the length of a measuring rod ahead of the sheriff and a baying mob. Myths are meant to be left alone.

Beyond Swansea you have the authentic Welsh heartland. There is a Semitic strength in the faces of the women and a fierce confidence in the eyes of the men, who hold enormous reservations about the conventions and laws that slip so smoothly down the gullet in other places. Go down to the Gower peninsula, a stretch of still and lovely places. Go down from Llandovery to Laugharne. (In Llandovery I actually went to sleep reading George Borrow in the room where George Borrow slept.)

In Laugharne you have a town of almost defiant calmness. Time in the quiet streets seems washed and harmless. There is a dead castle and a dead poet. On the slope above the hill, in the most Gothic churchyard I have ever seen, is the grave of Dylan Thomas, the sad, wild and wasted boyo, our archetypal talker and thinker.

In Laugharne I met a man who, for fifteen years, had been trying to arrange a meeting with Dylan. But Dylan's movements were as bewildering as his metaphors, and the pilgrim had never caught up with him. It was a dreary day; the drizzle was coming up from the estuary. The man stood by the grave, quite alone, and spoke out the lines of Dylan:

> Too late in the wrong rain
> They come together whom their love parted.

And all of a sudden the day's dreariness had gone. Anybody who can change the quality of rain from beyond the grave is an outsize in poets.

The journey from Carmarthen to Aberystwyth by train is one of the most reposeful stretches of railed track on earth. It has a calm so utter it would baffle a saint of quietness. There are hill prospects that exhaust every kind of mental music, and all around a sense of nature left unhurt and ungrudging. This is famous honey country. The railway company has a contract with the bees. The bees do not molest the passengers or try to scrounge free rides. The trains in return do not disturb the pollen.

At the salmon-heavy mouth of the Teifi is Cardigan Town. While charged with social vitality and charm for those who know it, it is no pleasure dome. But leading out of the town is a road of rare enchantment. The road dips and rises, articulately almost, as if warning you to expect something. At the top of the rise you gasp. Before you is the estuary of the Teifi, and the great promontories on either side, if the season be right, are two loud cries of yellow under the wild and muscular beauty of the flowering gorse.

166

The mind and eyes get the same kind of lift at the first view of Tenby, as you sweep around the last bend of the road from the north. The tavern doors still nod to you in apology for the Sabbath closure. It is as if the prickly edges of the Welsh conscience had been shaved smooth by the Mediterranean blue of its waters. On Caldey Island just off the coast, is the monastery established by the Brethren who survived the débâcle of Father Ignatius's abbey at Llanthony. The place has a magnetic charm. At the sight of it I felt the only recorded impulse in my life to be a monk.

It is a fair bet that if you mention Wales outside Wales, some, true to the tradition of the Romantic dreamers and escapers, would think of the mountains. It would not be a bad thought at that. Between Anglesey and the valley of the Taff the Ice Age did some of its subtlest bits of squeezing and moulding. Others, hearing Wales named, might snarl at the Welsh Sunday. And with reason, for this effort to bring us chastened and calm from Saturday to Monday is as confused and dispiriting a slap at sin as self-righteousness will ever record. But for the great majority, Wales will connote castles.

We have a lot of them and most of them merit a long look. The Normans put a great stone rump down on us, for we were a restless lot, always ready to come storming out of the hills to break our teeth and hearts against the nearest English bastion. It only took someone with a strong, buzzing Norman name like Fitzhugh or Fitzherbert to build a protective wall and in less time than it takes to shout ' *Ymlaen*' (forward) that wall was either wrapped around the neck of Fitzhugh or was being warmed by our bodies. But some of the stone stuck, and the castles rose in a land of scurrying, whispering, frowning folk who led vestigial lives in the distant hills until an Owen Glyndwr or a Prince Llewellyn or some other Welsh leader sang out once more and raised the banners for yet another bloody fling.

It is curious how fresh and immediate this ancient stuff can some-times be, especially in those northern ranges where the body of the land has come down from the Middle Ages virtually unchanged. Drive from the castle of Harlech to Machynlleth and time and again the hillsides seem to stir once more with the hosts of fierce, dark-faced men on their way to join their leader for a last raising of fists against the inclosing trap of English brain and muscle. The English trained on us. By the time they had us reeling wall-eyed around Snowdon and asking for the sponge in both languages, they were ready for Scotland, Ireland and Patrick Henry.

Owen Glyndwr died about 1415, a fugitive, unwilling to face the firm

Caerphilly Castle

but gentlemanly gibbet he might have expected from his pursuers. That was an unfair fate for the most dynamic leader of a people who derive such a strange enjoyment from funerals. We are not necrophiles but we tend to enjoy a public and dramatic release of compassion. And such ceremonies, with their mingling of the irreducibly private with the totally universal, give us a chance to talk at length. That we love. Reticence is the thing we really want to bury. Even our national emblematic vegetable, the leek, has a kind of vocal pungency about it.

An anatomy of Welsh castles would be fascinating to compile. Time and malice move at variable tempi. Some of the castles still stand, largely intact, significantly monstrous. The queen of them is Caernarvon in the north-west, and it still has a tenuous function in our contemporary political scene; each new Prince of Wales is proclaimed in its courtyard. Edward the First, who set an all-time record for killing Welshmen, instituted this solemn act in 1301 as part of the long process of saying he was sorry to have cut down so drastically on the singing, which even then was our favourite way of drying out after wars and monsoons.

The ceremonial proclamation robes, last worn in 1911 by the now Duke of Windsor, are to be seen in the National Museum of Wales in Cardiff. They are a masterwork in crimson velvet and ermine, a fair sight for the eyes of a nation so stubbornly prone to the wearing of blue serge. Soon, when Prince Charles will be admitted to his domain, the arrogant old pile at Caernarvon will become again a vast cup of heraldry and fanfare.

Caerphilly, in the south, balances Caernarvon like a massive book end. Its fabric dies, but slowly and with an almost audible defiance. The analogy is quite accurate. When you look at one of its towers that has broken away and now stands poised in half-collapse, you get an acute impression of laboured, painful breathing. As you run your fingers over the inner bones of those stricken walls, you have a rough digest of man's obdurate disunity. With people willing to take all that trouble to keep other people out, one guesses that man's progress has very largely been an exchange of caves.

The outer walls at Caerphilly bulge as if bursting with boredom at having to hang around so long. The lines of the great banqueting hall are superb and make one itch with misery that the authorities have not attempted a complete repair of this masterpiece of medieval racketeering. Owen Glyndwr started smashing the place up five hundred years ago, and in our time only a modest intervention by the Bute family and the Ministry of Works has prevented its utter dissolution.

Two masons are in perpetual residence doing fragmentary bits of conservation, and it is said that these two artisans chiseling away in their self-elected Bastille have become totally Norman in their responses; when they come down at day's end, crazed by loneliness and thirst for their evening pint, they look contumaciously at the townsmen.

To celebrate the Empire Games a couple of years ago, an attempt was made 'to replenish the ancient water defences', which is Caerphilly for filling the old moat. The water, on which desultory bits of boating and fishing take place, has a dull, lost look about it, as if failing to see the point of all this antiquarian archness. But it is a memorable and potently evocative survival all the same. Stand on the keep and stare at the surrounding hills, once alive with outraged and murderous bowmen edging in at nightfall on their tough, bandy legs, and you taste all the psychoses of siege and alienness.

On my last visit there a small boy was playing on one of the wall walks. His fancy was sunk deep in some Ivanhoe dream as he fired non-stop through the arrow slits, making with his mouth the zing of his invisible arrows. Then either he remembered some chore or his dream ran out of fuel. He called down to a man who was standing below, his eyes fixed on the West Gate to the Outer Ward. 'Hey, mister, what's the time?'

The man looked startled and pulled himself slowly from his own well-furnished reverie. He asked, 'What sort of a question is that to ask in a place like this?'

The boy said, 'Sorry,' as if he saw the man's point, whole and clear and sad.

The great majority of our castles were small affairs, easily kicked over and flattened. You can see them, whittled stumps, ivied little humps huddled in the middle of a wandering suburb or yielding to a cape of weeds on the edge of some utterly static hamlet, the drawn teeth of what was once as brazen a grin as the world has ever known, the clanking dominion of the potent hooligans who came out of the mists of the north to get warm and to make the world their parish.

No one bothers to sweep up these minute ruins. If anyone dared bull-doze them there would be a howl right through the land. Like junk in the attic they seem to help us preserve our frail sense of integrity. Alien and hostile as these forts have been in our national imagination, they are now part of our flesh, and we derive some sort of consolation from the elephantine thickness our conquerors thought fit to give their defences. Sometimes a large part of the fabric has been carted away by peasants in need of building material and only too delighted to cock a snook at their vanished overlords, as part of the historical process that culminated with Cromwell.

No man has ever brushed off a nation's past with as violent a contempt as Cromwell. He levelled the castles as if he saw them as galling obstructions in the innards of man's experience. As a rubble-maker he was almost in the same class as our own gentle astro-militarists in their quiet research rooms. You will see scores of his demolition jobs now nestling on the very lip of oblivion. Often they discharge pleasantly humdrum little functions, like serving to limit the range of some citizen's chicken run or vegetable patch.

From the base of a crumbling corner tower an indifferent hand throws maize or fertiliser where once a lover might have put his case with lute and aubade, and given the choice most people would still take eggs and potatoes. These squalid demotions from grace make a nice tickle on the nerve ends. On however sublime a level you may think you are communing with your soul, your passions or the universe, there is always some patient keeper of chickens or potatoes waiting for you to shut up or move on.

And between the great stranded petrifacts like Caernarvon and the mouldering toe bones of ancient glory like Penmark, near Cardiff, you have a few castles that have bustled up right into our own times with a picaresque vigour. In the 1930's William Randolph Hearst, who took up almost as many castles as Cromwell put down, moved into St Donat's on the Glamorgan coast looking out over the Tusker Rock, a tigerish reef that still chews up an astonishing number of craft yearly. Hearst had a beautiful cadence of gardens dropping down to the sea. He made a swimming pool out of the bare rock and did a fine job of sealing this part of the coast from the natives. If the latter failed to get the point from the many walls and hedges he put up, he had two seventeenth-century cannon mounted and polished to look as if they meant business.

We recalled Fitzhugh and Fitzherbert and stayed clear. According to the legend that Hearst swiftly knit around him, the swimming pool had a glass bottom below which there was a chamber where the inquisitive sybarites could sit, cricking their necks. Hearst built himself a snug little fief. The adjoining town of Llantwit Major still lives in a nervous thrill of vicarious raffishness when they recall the parties that came whooping into the Swan, the Globe, the White Hart from the castle.

Llantwit in the fourth and fifth centuries was one of the world's most eminent centres of learning. Princes came here from every corner of

Europe to sit at the feet of the early schoolmen. Today Llantwit is intellectually one of the least ambitious centres in the Western world. If princes came they would come only to sit and play darts, and if you ask any of the citizens for their proudest moments you will probably have pointed out to you some elder who saw Clark Gable or Marion Davies plain when, with a platoon of fellow revellers, they kicked up the biggest rumpus in the little town since the Danes last stormed up the beach in the eighth century.

I myself have been in St Donat's only twice. The first time was as a junior handler of sheet music to a noted male voice choir in the neighbourhood. Hearst was giving a stupendous party, at which one of the guests was that other ambivalent moralist, Lloyd George. He wanted to throw in something truly antiquarian short of shooting a couple of natives from the cannon. He had the choristers done up in white sheets to look like Druids and ordered them to shuffle through a grove of trees singing Welsh airs. I was not a singer but I qualified for a white sheet.

I have a memory of the moonlight in that grove and of thinking that Hearst had probably paid for a few extra beams. I recall finding myself more than once face down in that rich turf because I kept tripping over my robe, which had been made for a Druid four feet taller than myself. And notable as we turned the last corner of the grove was the sudden vision of golden repletion that burst forth from Hearst's lighted fortress. I have never felt properly oriented since.

The second occasion was a recent 'open day' when admission charges went to the local church fund. The swimming pool was jampacked with bobbing bodies and it would have taken a lean Cousteau to find whether or not the thing had a glass bottom. The gardens, classically made for meditation and romance, teemed with weary trippers baying for tea and buns. At the foot of the last gracious flight of steps taking us down to sea level, two striplings armed with switches were carefully denuding a spring-time bush of its bursting buds. Hearst would not have liked it. And for once the Vale of Glamorgan might conceivably have agreed with him.

Moving slightly to the east, on the side of the Taff, Castell Coch, Red Castle, rises suddenly from the trees. Its suggestion of a tooth-paste ad chimes oddly with the fact that it stands on the threshold of valleys made carious with industrial refuse. On its site was once the fortress of Ifor Bach, Little Ivor, a bow-legged battler, a master of ambush who kept the nerves of the Normans scalloped. The Norman overlord at Cardiff, sick of Ifor, abducted the Welshman's young bride. Ifor and his men tunnelled their way from Castell Coch into Cardiff Castle, a long enough journey even on a municipal bus. He recovered his bride.

The overlord called up reserves from the border country and mounted a counter-sweep. Ifor fled into the Rhondda hills. The cavalcade of vindictive warriors clanked up into the mountains behind him. In the trees, at a spot where the Taff's banks stretch back to form a pleasant meadow, Ifor lay in wait with his friends, whom he had called to his side with beacon fires that had burned for fifty miles around. The Normans paused to rest. The arrows of the hillmen poured down. The fact of death was great in the valley and the tears of the Norman women were deep.

More Normans came, more ruthless and wary. Ifor perished. His fortress was destroyed. Five hundred years later the Marquis of Bute re-created the castle as a hunting lodge and a place of retreat for his friends. Edward VII and his grandson both slept there. They might have slept on a bed which can still be seen there, an article with ornate glass knobs which would have puzzled Ifor Bach, even after all that tunnelling.

There is an impression outside Wales that the Welsh are a grimly religious people. This is not exact. The belief was given strength by the great gallery of ferociously hypocritical deacons to be found in Welsh writing since 1910 or so, from Caradoc Evans onwards. Caradoc seems never to have known a deacon poised for any programme other than to flush the sexual coverts of his village, a specialised myopia that once had him haring away from a posse of peasants with pitchforks.

It is the old story of a deeply sensual and ardent but poor people needing the cooling robe of an outward piety to cut down expenses and to keep the glands stable. In various of the dimmer-lit, rain-shot, slate-veined villages of the north you might get a taste of the dourness you still get in full midnight bloom in parts of Scotland, but in Wales as a whole you rarely fail to find hints of a roistering levity.

For the last three centuries we have had waves of religious revivalism of volcanic force. I have a theory about them. In our unregenerate days we must have kept life in such an uproar with our licentious revelry, we kept the whole of Europe awake. So we were told to shut up. A shock brigade of austere nay-sayers stood by to purge us of gaiety, to silence our laughter and hamstring our host of leaping lovers. A wind of wrath had our guilt feelings standing at attention and saluting. Our hot cheeks were cooled with a widening fan of hymnals.

The most dramatic and memorable of these jehads was in 1904. From a hamlet in Cardiganshire came an astonishingly handsome young man, Evan Roberts. For one short summer his tongue blazed through the land. Not a single conscience, counting out a few obdurate tipplers stuck away in the remoter clefts, was unsinged. To this day, tough old miners single out that strange burst of summer rapture as the one luminous hour in long, greyish lives.

And to legions of women, excited by his images into a vision of a million doors opening all over the earth, he remained the unforgettable paladin of a life raised for an instant above littleness and tedium. At the end of his brief mission he withdrew into silence; not back to his native hamlet but to an English city, Derby. A disturbing and very Welsh tale altogether, a characteristic Cambrian grafting of Mohammed and Valentino. But we must add a rider; neither of the two candent masters mentioned did the course in so short a time as Roberts.

Pembrokeshire is the logical last stage in any view of Wales. The main mountain range of that county, the Prescellys, may not have the indigo grandeur of Snowdon and her sisters, but it has the controlled and manageable beauty that runs like a theme through the lands hemmed by the Severn Channel and Cardigan Bay. No subtler succession of green delights can ever be found than on the road from St Dogmael's in the north to Milford Haven in the south. Half-way, at St David's, our patron saint left his great sweet memory and his few small bones.

And humanly, few places in Wales are more interesting. The northern half of the county is occupied by people whose first language is Welsh. In the south, settled largely by people of Huguenot descent, any mention of the old Celtic tongue is likely to get a black look. So the Welsh of North Pembrokeshire have taken on a sense of being different which has led to some strange mental results.

This is the region nearest in feel and spirit to Ireland, to the acceptance of a rather whimsical supernatural world complementary to our own. Many of the people claim to be fey, able at enormous distances to anticipate or instantly to share the anguish or joy of those they love. A careless seaman on the meat run to South America has his head banged by a swinging hoof on a wharf in Buenos Aires. His wife screams compassionately at precisely that moment in the village of Boncath.

I can think of nothing more wearing than those suprasensory bouts of pity and alarm. Take the legend of the 'corpse candles'. Those whose sympathy gives them a third eye claim that they can see a phantom light rising from the house of one who is shortly to die, and the light makes its way to the graveyard. This created a lot of genuine confusion among the air-raid wardens of Pembrokeshire, who were trying to enforce a total black-out during the early stages of the last war. When they would imagine that a curtain of blackness lay over the land, some fey special constable would start seeing a whole series of ambulant, premonitory flickers. The finish of it was that they had to weed out of the force all officers whose night vision was not sombrely normal.

One seeks the moment of recollection through which a land and a people can express their own essential face and voice. One such for me is a journey I made from Holyhead in North Wales right down to Barry on the Bristol Channel, Wales's frontier in the south. I was returning with a busload of baritones, a velvet cohort, members of a male choral group. We were on our way back from an eisteddfod. We had paused in mid-evening near Cader Idris. We ate an imperial meal of bacon, cheese and onion, very much a dish of the country, and we laved it down with a benediction of strong, nut-brown ale. We re-entered the bus and headed south. Song rose from a well of cheese and ale and genial pity, and the sound of the harmonies was as passionate and poignant as the purple serrations of the twilit mountains ahead.

Above Cwm Bychan, Merioneth